MONTANA
WATERING HOLES
The Big Sky's Best Bars

JOAN MELCHER

gpp

Guilford, Connecticut

Text design: Libby Kingsbury
Layout: Lisa Reneson
Project manager: John Burbidge
Map: Melissa Baker © Morris Book Publishing, LLC
Interior photos: © Kurt Keller

Library of Congress Cataloging-in-Publication Data
Melcher, Joan.
 Montana watering holes : the Big Sky's best bars / Joan Melcher.
   p. cm.
 Includes bibliographical references.
 ISBN 978-0-7627-4948-5
 1. Bars (Drinking establishments)—Montana—Guidebooks. 2. Montana—Guidebooks. I. Title.
 TX950.57.M9M45 2009
 647.959786—dc22

                                      2009022413

Printed in the United States of America

10 9 8 7 6 5 4 3 2 1

It was Sunday night. I had hoped the saloons would stay open long enough for me to see them. They never even closed. In a great old-time saloon I had a giant beer. On the wall was a big electric sign-board flashing gambling numbers. . . . What characters in there: old prospectors, gamblers, whores, miners, Indians, cowboys, tobacco-chewing businessmen! Groups of sullen Indians drank rotgut in the john. Hundreds of men played cards in an atmosphere of smoke and spittoons. It was the end of my quest for an ideal bar. . . .

—◆—

Jack Kerouac
writing about Butte's M&M bar in *Esquire* magazine, 1970

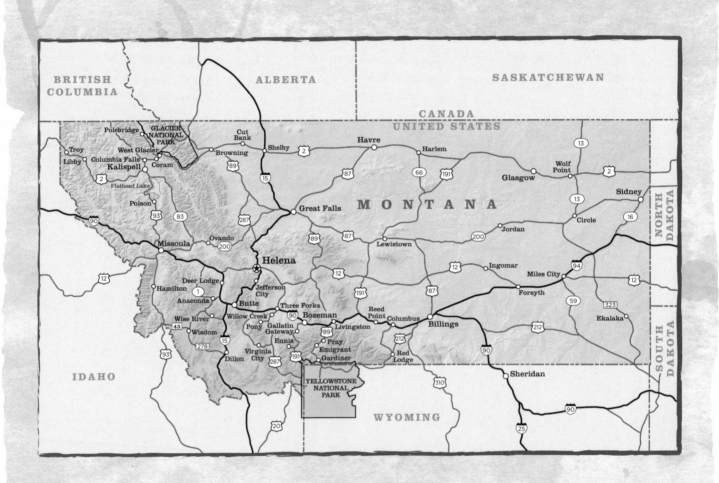

CONTENTS

INSTITUTIONS OF IMPORTANCE

It is rather astonishing that an institution as important as the western bar should have almost entirely escaped the attention of historians. It may be that historians have simply made the a *priori* judgment that people went to bars merely to carouse and shoot each other.

More probably, the subject has been largely ignored because the material for research simply isn't there—or is so sparse as to render serious study almost impossible. . . . Historians are constantly adjured not to "read the present into the past." But like all academic adjurations, this one should be taken with a generous measure of salt. . . .

If you thumb through this book cursorily you will conclude that it is a commentary on today's saloons in various Montana cities—saloons both old and new, west and east—that it is a well-written, humorous, and sympathetic treatment. In a way it is a kind of guide to Montana's most interesting saloons. And it makes you want to visit them and see for yourself.

But if you sit down and give this book a little solid attention, you will find that it is a great deal more than a once-over-lightly guidebook. Joan Melcher has subtly ignored the rule "do not read today into yesterday." She has done this with profit to history and with skill and sensitivity. It is clear that in certain basic respects the role of the western saloon remains what it has always been. As an institution of importance it has always had its detractors—indeed it has always been venomously attacked by the pious and the righteous. The attacks have never really mattered to the keepers of the institutions nor to the patrons. The western saloon is simply too important a social, economic, and political instrument of western society to be turned aside from its predestined course. This is an intriguing, funny, and, mark you, important book.

—The late K. Ross Toole, Hammond Professor of Western History,
University of Montana, writing in the Foreword to the first edition

PREFACE

Years ago, in what now seems to have been my infancy but was really my twenties, I wrote a book about Montana bars. Then I purported to go on a search for the "perfect Montana bar." Of course, we all know perfection is defined by what likely cannot be achieved, so although the trip was fruitful in many ways, it was in essence a quixotic trek along Montana's backroads and interstate highways with the "perfect" bar always over the horizon, beyond reach, elusive, beckoning—the reason to jump in my 1976 Renault one more time and head out for a new adventure. That book was defined by and dedicated to the bartenders, a rich brew of all that has made Montana great—Bob Gohn, blind grandson of a Montana vigilante and a Virginia City miner, boxing legend Sonny O'Day, Butte's community stalwart Charley Judd, Kalispell's Moose Miller, the Jersey Lilly's Bill Sewart, the Club Cigar's Lena Ford. That book gave me great pleasure, a little notoriety in the state, and my first brush with the publishing business. It was a coming-of-age book and after a few years was only a line at the bottom of my resumé. But a fondness for the subject remained, and I was always pleased when I'd be in a bar and someone would say, "Are you the one who wrote the book?"

When an editor from a publishing house approached me about updating the search a few years ago, I was flattered, interested, and a little scared. My first thought was about all the legendary bartenders I had met before and would not be able to visit again. I wondered if today's proprietors could be anywhere near as interesting. And I thought about how poker and keno machines had made their way into most bars, even the well-preserved turn-of-the-century saloons. I worried that they would have made such an impact as to render social interaction and the Montana bar's role as a community gathering spot obsolete—or at least lessen it to a disturbing degree. I wondered if the Montana bar was still playing myriad roles in the culture of the state. I had many questions that could be answered only by another search, another series of adventures.

Not many writers have the opportunity to revisit their earlier works. Change is inevitable, and can be disturbing, especially if what you've written about before was, for the most part, pleasing to you. But at the same time, it is a unique opportunity to place oneself and the object of study in a new perspective. Travel writer and novelist Paul Theroux retraced much of a trip by rail through Europe, the Middle East, Asia, and Russia (first written about in *The Great Railway Bazaar*) thirty-three years later in a marvelous book, *Ghost Train to the Eastern Star* (Houghton Mifflin: 2008). In an introduction he noted travel writers who had never returned to the place they had become known for writing about, including Graham Greene, Evelyn Waugh, Charles Darwin, and more:

> *Eric Newby went down the Ganges once, Jonathan Raban down the Mississippi once, and Jan Morris climbed Everest once. Robert Byron did not take the road to Oxiana again, Cherry-Garrard made only one trip to Antarctica, Chatwin never returned to Patagonia, nor did Doughty go back to Arabia Deserta, nor Wallace to the Malay Archipelago, nor Waterton to the Amazon, nor Trollope to the West Indies, nor Edward Lear to Corsica, nor Stevenson to the Cévennes, nor Chekhov to Sakhalin, nor Gide to the Congo, nor Canetti to Marrakesh, nor Jack London to the Solomon Islands, nor Mark Twain to Hawaii.*

He goes on to note a few authors who did return—Henry Morton Stanley, who recrossed Africa ten years after his first trip, and Richard Henry Dana, who returned to San Francisco in 1864, twenty-four years after his 1840 visit to find that "it had changed from a gloomy Spanish mission station with a few shacks to an American boom town that had been transformed by the Gold Rush." The fact that Theroux decided to retrace his first trip was an effort he noted Woodsworth and Yeats attempted by returning to an earlier landscape of their lives. He said writing about travel had become a way of making sense of his life.

I don't intend to put myself in such notable literary company—Theroux included—but this book is in some ways a travel book and as such my revisiting earlier haunts may shed light on what Montana was then and is now. It may act as a sort of social barometer. How are we doing? Are we still talking civilly to our neighbors? Helping the down and out? Tending to our oral traditions? Being fair? Welcoming strangers? Saving our history? Having fun?

You'll find this book is a duet of past and present; a melody line cradled in chords usually harmonic, sometimes dissonant. I determined to visit all of the bars listed in my first book and to add a few new ones. Material from the first book would be used to compare past and present and keep alive the spirit of the bars that are gone.

Many times I found I could settle into a bar like I had hardly left it; other times I was shocked to my toenails—not because the bar was so much different, but because it was not as I remembered it and had counted on it staying. Nostalgia is a key part of Montanans' attachments to bars; we began writing our history not long after we arrived and settled this land and sometimes it seems we place too much emphasis on the past. Some may see that as shortsighted, myopic, dangerously parochial. But I would counter that it's more a parallel course—that history runs with us and acts as a touchstone, a guide, a way of viewing today and the next, remembering where we were in order to decide where we'll go tomorrow.

Our saloons, as repositories of fragments of our early days, are key to that intrinsic memory. I knew going into this adventure that, for me, a successful outcome would be that I would find the bars had changed little, that they were still community gathering spots, holders of unlikely stories, welcoming outposts, stalwart isles in the eddies of twenty-first-century change. And I'm happy to report that, for the most part, I was not disappointed.

Many things have changed in my life, of course. I am nearly thirty years older; I have wrinkles, blood pressure pills, and a bigger waistline. Instead of an almost new car, I drive a ten-year-old Volkswagen Jetta. Gas on the first trip cost around seventy-five cents a gallon; I was paying more than four dollars a gallon during the summer of 2008. In those days I used an IBM Selectric typewriter and thought I was tech savvy. Today I use an iMac that can do things I don't even know about. Before, my father was a U.S. Senator and writing the book was in a small way a rebellious act, payback for the scrutiny his prominence had rained down on my siblings and myself. This time he accompanied me to a couple of the bars.

Before, when freelance jobs began to dry up, I took a full-time job, squeezing out weekends and vacation time for more travel. This time I'd just left a job and squeezed bar trips into my freelance schedule. Before, I had two sedentary cats and a few friends willing to accompany me on the bar search; often I set off on my own. This time I had more friends up for the adventure—and a life partner and a dog—and rarely went alone. Before, I was writing on speculation and took two years to complete the project; this time I had a publisher, an advance, and a tighter timeframe.

What can I say, nearly seven thousand miles later? I was grateful to find some of the same people I had interviewed in the 1970s were still behind the plank—Charlotte and Dick Sapa in Columbia Falls; John Tovin in Great Falls; Diana Hahn in Reed Point. I was heartened to learn of some great saloons I had missed before or that hadn't been in existence then—the Sip 'n Dip in Great Falls, the Bulldog in Whitefish, the Willow Creek Cafe and Saloon.

Like before, I developed something of an escape reflex; often I'd find myself itching to throw a few days' clothes into my purple sachel and hit the road. I'd come back energized, with new stories to tell, old legends to put in perspective, fresh images of long-held customs. There was always another bar on the horizon.

It's true that I missed the old bartenders, especially toward the end of my search. They were characters who cannot be replaced, and they formed the backbone of the first book. Unique icons from a time when western individualism meant, for those creative men and women, carving a wide swath and standing square in the middle of it—Luigi with his twinkling lights, melodious pipes, and sardonic one-liners; Sonny O'Day, the Italian boxer with the Irish name who had drawn Cassius Clay and Sonny Preston to Laurel to tend bar with him; John Quigley, who created his own town out of rock and wood; Trixi, who retired graciously from an international career of trick roping to lasso a region into her saloon and restaurant. Many of the bartenders I found this time around were employees, gracious but without the depth of experience and knowledge of their bar and their town.

That said, I was happy to find some new folks carrying on the tradition of the iconic Montana bartender: people such as Buck May at the Bulldog in Whitefish, Scott and Paula at the Pony Bar in Pony, and Wally and Laurie Abrisson at the Longbranch in Ennis. No doubt, there's been a little unraveling of the fabric of the Montana saloon, but it's still there and it's still whole.

If you're reading this book, you know how a friend's face lights up when you tell him you've recently stopped at one of his haunts. They're often remote outposts like the Jersey Lilly in Ingomar or the Northern Lights in Polebridge, but it could also be Butte's M&M, Miles City's Montana Bar, Missoula's Charlie B's, or a little-known nook on the Hi-Line.

Before long you'll be hearing stories about the place and the people who frequent it, another fragment of an oral history that is part and parcel of how Montana came to be and how it views the future. These places are part of our bloodstream. Of course, many of our favorite bars are little holes in the wall not likely to be featured here simply because there had to be some criteria for inclusion. My criteria, generally, was to include saloons recognized by the broader community of Montanans as classic watering holes or intrinsic community gathering spots. But I would never contend that this is a definitive collection of the "best" bars in Montana. As I was finishing this manuscript a story in a newspaper described a bar that had changed with new owners, the Frenchtown Club. A local heralded the change—"You come in in a bad mood, and they'll get you out of it"—and although the writer of the story said there was nothing out of the ordinary about the place, the regulars—who know—deem it a "real Montana bar." There's not much more to add to that.

In a film on his favorite bars titled *The Way of the Road*, James Crumley concluded, "The perfect Montana bar is probably the one you're sitting in at the moment." He was right. It is that sense of coming home that poet Richard Hugo wrote about in "The Only Bar in Dixon." William Kittredge described it in an ode to bars and escape, an essay called *"Drinking and Driving"*: "We learn it early in the West, drinking and driving, chasing away from the ticking stillness of home toward some dim aura, glowing over the horizon, call it possibility or excitement." The journey, the search, is all. Finding is a very personal arrival. Hugo pegged it as well as anyone, writing about his once-favorite bar in Bonner: "You were nothing going in but now you kiss your hand."

Last time I ended my introduction noting how, as I was finishing the manuscript, more people approached me about different bars that I hadn't made it to. I noted then how I had run out of time, that it was time to throw the reins to the readers to let them continue the search. I feel the same way today. We've come full circle. It's your turn. God speed.

And cheers!

FELLOW BAR HOPPERS

Thanks to those who accompanied me on the search. In order of appearance: Kelly Spears, Bailey, John D. Melcher, Simone Ellis, Michelle Lande, Lenny Lande, Jerry Boland, Dianne Carlson, John C. Melcher, Jill Melcher, Gena Ruth Thompson, Courtney Ellis, Peg Long, Deborah Hanson, Terry Hanson, and Dave Velasquez.

BEING ENTERTAINED BY STRANGERS

One cold spring evening in the mid-1970s, a tiring day of travel behind me, I pulled abruptly up to a bar on the outskirts of West Glacier, Montana. I needed a bracer and a change of position after four days on the road.

I sipped my burgundy, as comfortable as I would have been in my own kitchen, and watched happy hour in West Glacier. Two couples were drinking beer, bantering with the bartender. No one spoke to me—the audience—but I laughed along with the jokes.

The bartender whispered aside to me that the mayor of the town was coming. The door squeaked slowly open, letting in the damp of rain and cold, and Old Tim shuffled comfortably in, an old wool hat pulled tightly down over an old Irish head. He took a stool near mine. Tim's maxim for the night, mumbled in a raspy brogue, was "Ah, just keep a cool head and a dry back, and you'll be just fine."

The regulars and I agreed it was not bad advice, and while they shot pool, I contemplated my good fortune. Having stopped along the road at an unknown tavern, I had found laughter, wine to warm my insides and relax my stiffened limbs, companionship from people I couldn't call by name, and even a bit of country philosophy from an old Irishman who had worked the mines in Butte. I had found the Montana bar—the social sanctuary of the West.

INTRODUCTION:
A Select History of Montana Bars

Montana's first bar probably was no more than a plank of wood laid across two whiskey kegs. It might have been set up on a mountain pass by a prospector who used his grubstake to buy a supply of whiskey to sell to weary travelers. Or perhaps it was the first countertop of an enterprising merchant who brought a stock from the East to sell to trappers in the Northwest Territory. The first bartender may have been an itinerant whose purpose was to raise enough money to get to the next gold strike. Or he may have been a hardworking young man who would later achieve wealth and community stature. He may even have been a she, although the small percentage of women in Montana in those early days makes that unlikely.

One thing we know for certain. The famed plank was here shortly after people were. Eventually, the plank and kegs were covered by a tent. Tacked on the front of the canvas often was a hand-lettered sign heralding what lay within. Historical photographs show tent saloons in several Montana towns, often with a proud proprietor posing outside.

The tent saloon was crude and makeshift in comparison to the elaborate saloons that were to proliferate in the latter part of the nineteenth century. But there were few solid structures of any sort in early day Montana. A tent was a luxury to men who rarely slept with anything but stars overhead. Often the tent saloon was the main mercantile in town. And when optimism in the cow towns and mining camps reached a fevered pitch and men began erecting solid structures, the saloon was often the first.

Back bars and accompanying saloon fixtures were sent from points East up the Missouri by steamboat to Fort Benton. Beginning in the 1860s this inland waterway was to play a key role in the settlement of Montana and an even more important role in the territory's social life. It opened the door to an era of shining mahogany, gleaming mirrors, brass foot rails, and the veiled ladies in gilded frames.

SOCIAL SANCTUARY

Montana was settled by single men—adventurers, drifters, opportunists, fugitives from the law. Many had left comfortable livelihoods in the East on the gamble of untold wealth. Others were compulsive drifters whose glance invariably turned to greener pastures. Some were young romantics; others, no doubt, lawless misfits. Many were veterans of the Civil War—Confederate as well as Union soldiers—who carried their enmity to new ground. Many had come to Montana by way of gold or silver camps in Arizona, Nevada, Colorado, and New Mexico.

These men met with a more beautiful, yet hostile nature than they probably had ever known, often going for days or weeks without seeing another human being. The mining camps and trailheads, as tenuous as they were, offered as much "civilization" as they were to find.

They must have been, at times, lonely, depressed, afraid, smitten with severe cases of cabin fever. For all the obvious reasons, they needed to drink. But there were countless other reasons they frequented the saloon.

In the absence of any other gathering spot, the saloon was town hall, church, livery stable, hotel, cafe, theater, reading room, election hall, stage stop, and bank.

Wakes, weddings, funerals, and baptisms were held in the saloon. Wandering minstrels found a ready stage there. Accommodating bartenders held a miner's poke and were trusted more than the bankers who were to arrive much later. Newcomers to the camp were allowed to sleep on the floor of a saloon until other accommodations were available. Elections were held there, as well as church services. Major community decisions were made in the saloon, as well as business transactions that were to affect a territory the size of four eastern states. Later, journalists would be given expense accounts for the saloon, considered a prime source for news leads. And regardless of what they tell you, there was such a thing as a free lunch—in the early day saloon.

That plank of wood laid across kegs was to become the social sanctuary of the West.

In *Saloons of the Old West*, historian Richard Erdoes enumerates the many roles of the western saloon:

The saloon was all things to all men. Besides being a drinking place, it was an eatery, a hotel, a bath and comfort station, a livery stable, gambling den, dance hall, bordello, barbershop, courtroom, church, social club, political center, dueling ground, post office, sports arena, undertaker's parlor, library, news exchange, theater, opera, city hall, employment agency, museum, trading post, grocery, ice cream parlor, even a forerunner of the movie house, in which entranced cowhands cranked the handles of ornate kinetoscopes to watch the jerky movements of alluring cancan dancers. It has been jokingly said that, with the exception of the Battle of the Little Bighorn, all western history was made inside the saloons, and there is a grain of truth in this.[1]

An anthropologist who studied four saloons in the boomtown era of Virginia City, Nevada, came to the same conclusion. In *Boomtown Saloons: Archaeology and History in Virginia City,* Kelly Dixon describes the findings of a dig that sought to determine the social lives and interactions of people living in the boomtown in the latter half of the nineteenth century.

Dixon notes the western myth of violence in the saloons of the Old West—perpetrated by the wide-eyed eastern press along with "Hollywood-induced imagery about cowboys, gunfighters, and brawls"—was far from what her findings indicate:

> *...nineteenth-century media audiences were fed a wilder West than the one of reality. So how can archaeology help us adjust the inaccurate picture of violence in western saloons? Along with an abundance of beverage bottles, artifacts such as tobacco pipes, dice, poker chips, a cribbage board, and dominoes answer this question, demonstrating that saloons were primarily places for people to amuse themselves while enjoying a drink and relaxing with a smoke.... Given the leisure connotations of such artifacts, their presence reminds us that people attended saloons for the most part to relax and socialize, not to find or cause trouble.*[2]

ALL THE MAJOR DECISIONS

The decision to apply for territorial status for Montana was reached by a group of Montana pioneers passing a Sunday afternoon in a Bannack saloon, according to one account. Reportedly John Con Orem, famed pugilist, blacksmith, and saloon owner, was among the group, as was Sidney Edgerton, who was to be named the first territorial governor.

The distance of Lewiston (Idaho), then capital of the territory, was a sore point among Montana settlers. Orem, in one of his many Sunday-afternoon oratories in this particular saloon, called for seeking territorial status. Soon after, petitions were circulated among the mining camps and a collection of gold dust was taken to pay Edgerton's way to Washington. The news came of Edgerton's success:

> *Much gold was pinched from pokes in Bannack saloons that night. Everyone felt they were making history, as they were for that matter. Bannack, the glory of which was beginning to wane on account of strikes that were being made in Alder Gulch and elsewhere, took on a new lease on life.... Then Virginia City, much larger than Bannack, decided that she wanted the capitol, and took it.... More gold dust was pinched from gold pokes in the saloons of Bannack that night by way of consolation.*[3]

Bannack was not only to lose the capital to a booming Virginia City, but also her favorite son. Con Orem was to establish the Champion Saloon in Virginia City, where he easily combined his pugilistic career with saloon life. Advertisements that appeared in the *Montana Post* in 1864 hailed Orem's saloon as "adorned with the best set of sporting pictures west of New York" and added: "Private Lessons in boxing and sparring once a week."

Once Montana became a territory, it was quick to exercise jurisprudence. Montana's first trial took place in 1862 in Hell Gate at Bolt's Saloon.[4]

FIGHTS AND FIGHTS ABOUT FIGHTS

Sporting events were promoted heavily through the saloon, and Orem was to figure in many of the noteworthy promotions of early day Montana. A fighting hero to the miners of the camp, Orem occasionally came out from behind the bar to meet a challenger. One fight was to go down in history. It matched Orem with Irishman Hugh O'Neil; the men fought 185 rounds, from evening until dawn, when the referee finally called the match a draw. Another fight was to last even longer. One historian writes of this running fight about a fight:

Perhaps the most famous drinking argument in history is one that raged in American saloons for nearly three-quarters of a century. That basic dispute concerns whether Custer and his troops were drunk the night before their battle. Many Indians claimed they were—that was why the Indians decided to fight. A man espoused the "drunk" theory in a saloon in Helena one night. Another patron accused the man of mental clumsiness, then called him a known thief of soiled garments of blind laundry girls and the fight was on . . .[5]

Then there were the fights of a more spontaneous nature:

When Forsyth, Montana, was the end of the line on the Northern Pacific, twelve saloons arrived in sections, each with the conventional bar, beer cooler, table and piano. "The bartender" in one joint was setting out the drinks before the roof was on, the professor was spanking the ivories, and in a matter of hours a man had already been shot in an argument over a dance hall girl.[6]

Fights and killings were clearly part of the early Montana saloon. But even the most celebrated of male bastions had its domestic side. A sign in an early Helena saloon admonished: DON'T FORGET TO WRITE DEAR MOTHER. SHE IS THINKING OF YOU. WE FURNISH PAPER AND ENVELOPES FREE AND HAVE THE BEST WHISKEY IN TOWN.

☞ The Montana Bar in Miles City, like many Montana bars, has been a social sanctuary for more than one hundred years.

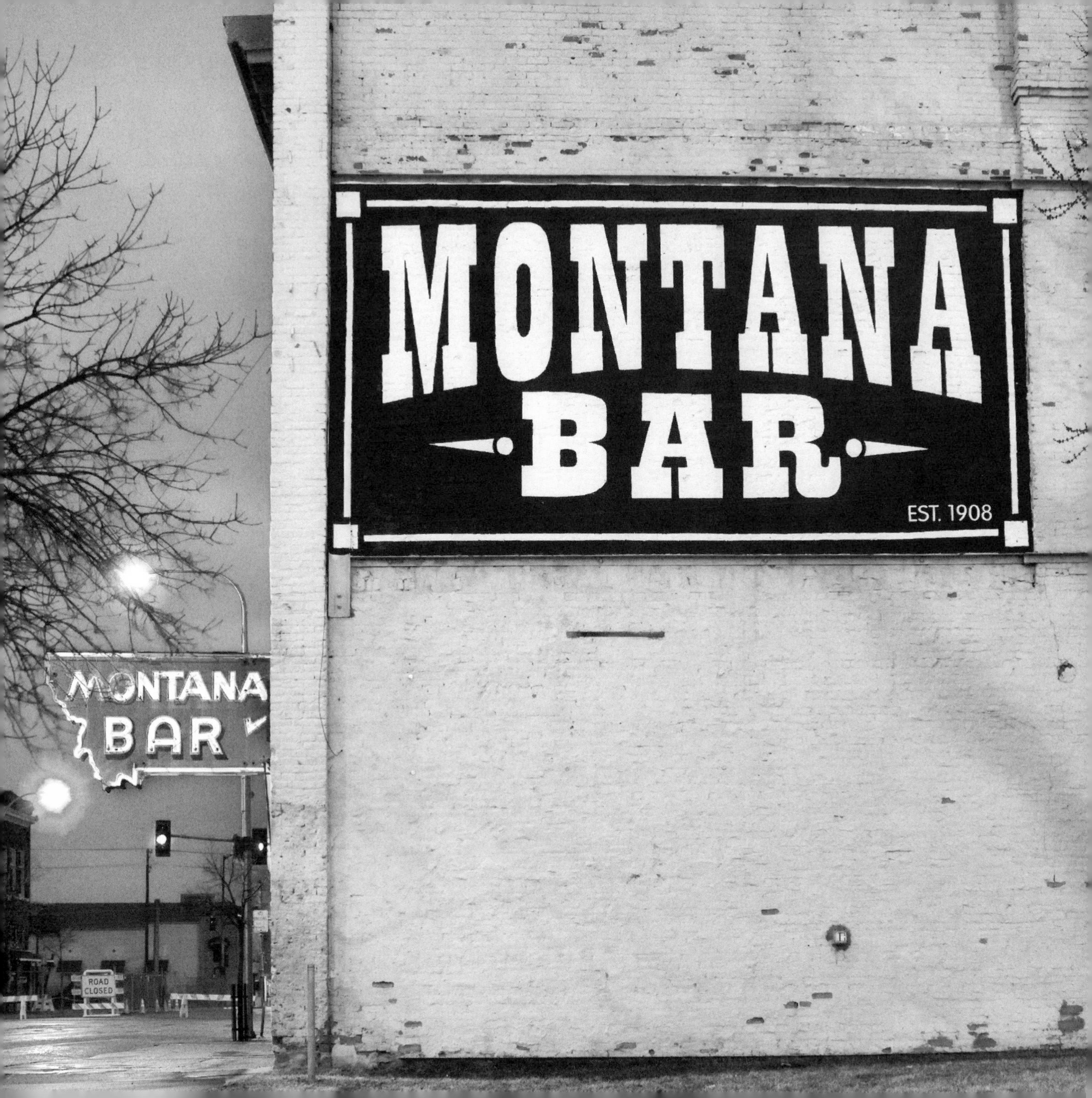
MONTANA
BAR
EST. 1908
MONTANA
BAR
ROAD
CLOSED

BARTENDERS, VAGRANTS, AND CELEBRITIES

The bartenders of the early days were often some of the best-liked and most respected citizens of the community. An early settler, Samuel William Carvoso Whipps, gives testimony to the good-heartedness of a couple of early Montana bartenders in the March 25, 1867, entry to his diary. Whipps had lived in various towns in Montana before this day, which found him in Livingston:

One day I stepped into a saloon to get a bottle of whiskey. Much to my surprise this place was run by my old friend of Sidney days, Joe Lane, who ran the dance hall. He, his woman Old Em, and Calamity Jane were there. Had I been their long lost son they could not have been gladder to see me. All of these people of the class usually condemned by preachers were big-hearted, generous people. Calamity Jane was noted for her kindness and generosity to the down and outs. She would divide her last crumb with them. A peculiar woman, generally wearing men's clothing, she was a noted and successful gambler and quick on the trigger, like poor old Jerry Phillips, who ran the most notorious place ever in Kalispell. . . . Both helped with money and fed thousands of down and outs.[7]

Another account showed a generosity beyond the pale:

D.H. Edmonds in his reminiscences about life in early Montana wrote about Joe the Barkeep, an ex-cowpuncher who would always help a down-and-out cowboy, supplementing each loan with a quart of the hard stuff and a Colt .45 wrapped in a towel—the "traveling kit."[8]

Bartenders sometimes took trade for a liquor bill, often as a last resort; sometimes the trade was more than fair:

Charles Russell was a forty-dollar-a-month cowhand when he traded his paintings for drinks at his friend Sid Willis' Mint Saloon at Great Falls, Montana. To other saloons he charged ten dollars per picture. One bartender promised him seventy-five dollars a month "and grub" for a whole year's output of paintings and sketches, establishing this saloon keeper as a patron of the arts. His offer, after all, amounted to more than double the wages Russell earned as a competent cowboy. One of Russell's oldest friends said later that the saloon owners were the first to recognize Charlie's genius and that there was no difference in quality between the pictures he sold for ten dollars in saloons and those he later sold for ten thousand dollars in New York.[9]

The saloon attracted its share of vagrants. But it was one of a few, if not the only, public structures in a camp. It provided most of the basic services, including the most basic—shelter from the cold and the heat.

THE THEATER

But if bartenders had to contend with vagrants and troublemakers, they also rubbed elbows with some of the more successful men and women of their time. One saloon in Butte—the Orpheum—was known to host the big-name performers who played in Butte during the town's heyday. Pictures of celebrities crowded the walls of the Orpheum, wrote a Butte journalist in 1919, adding that visiting celebrities would stop by "to see if their picture was still on the wall or donate one to the collection."

The journalist talked of one of the more celebrated of Orpheum patrons: "Chaplin pretty nearly lived in the place the week he was in the vaudeville play *A Night in a London Music Hall.* . . . We put on many a show that was better than the one you saw on the stage. . . ." [10]

In the cow town of Miles City, the theatrical experience was a little more rough-hewn:

> . . . the first theatrical performance—Uncle Tom's Cabin— was given inside Charlie Brown's saloon on an improvised stage made of planks supported by beer and whiskey barrels. As Elizah fled from the bloodhounds she stumbled, dislodged a board, and fell amid rolling kegs. [11]

Saloon keepers no doubt benefited by staging performances in their establishments, and few in the mining camps or nascent cow towns wanted to miss the show:

> When a theater opened in a Helena saloon, the sheriff and his deputies did not want to miss out and consequently had to take their only prisoner, a Flathead Indian, along. All went well until the actors started killing each other on stage and the frightened prisoner, who took the stabbings for real, nose-dived screaming through a window, jumped on a horse, and was never seen again. [12]

Dancing was a common thread that introduced a broad swath of women to the saloon. Hurdy-gurdy halls spread from the mining camps to cow towns:

> In 1865, in Montana mining settlements, the hurdy-gurdy was a most popular place, and when Montana became cattle country, the cowboys put their own brand on the dance saloons. In a Billings watering hole a puncher and a waitress took first prize for dancing the "Bull Calf's Medley" on the grand piano at a gala Saturday night hoedown. The cowboy wore high boots which did the piano no good, and the exuberant onlookers kept discharging their six-guns at the ceiling to the beat of waltzes and polkas. [13]

THE FREE LUNCH

The free lunch was a common enticement to drink in many of the early saloons, and accounts of the victuals range from peanuts in the shell to oysters on the half shell. For a short time in bar history, it was the main sustenance of many. Many old-timers remember how the free lunch carried them through lean times. Miles City bartender Charlie Brown was known to keep a pot of mulligan stew on the stove twenty-four hours a day for hungry customers. [14]

But it was in Butte that the free lunch reached its full potential. An article in the January 4, 1892, *Montana Standard* first chastised the vagrants who took advantage of the free lunch and then went on to describe, in mouthwatering detail, the delicacies offered. The headline of the story declared: How Hundreds of Lazy Men Secure a Free Meal; a subhead reiterated: Bums and Vags Who Believe That the World Owes Them a Living—What They Eat.

The story described the free-lunch circuit in Butte: "There are half a dozen saloons in the city each of which gets up more things to eat free than the two best hotels in Butte at any price." The reporter himself obviously had indulged. He listed several saloons and the bills of fare for which they were famous, including lobster, roast pig, imported sausages, sardines, herrings, and oysters on the half shell.

The saloon, like an old but spry vaudevillian with a trunk full of masks, was to change its identity constantly. When it wasn't serving some of the best food in town, it was hosting a prizefight, counting ballots from a camp election, staging a play, or witnessing the baptizing of a baby.

SERVICES

The saloon's role as church is one of its most interesting incarnations. Weddings, funerals, baptisms—all were performed in the saloon, to say nothing of weekly services. One historian claims bartenders encouraged preachers to hold services in their establishments because their customers' enthusiasm in worship was quickly converted to enthusiasm for the bottle.[15]

An account of one of many traveling ministers to find haven in a saloon is attributed to a bar in Wyoming, but no doubt was typical of similar occurrences in Montana.

In one Wyoming camp, an itinerant preacher entered a saloon asking the owner if he could hold a sermon in the place. The saloon keeper assented immediately. The drinking customers and gamblers roared their hearty approval and offered help. The bartender's arrangements were most satisfactory. Sheets were strung on a wire to "shut out the sight of the bar." Extra chairs and benches were borrowed from neighbors to seat all comers. A sturdy table was put in one corner. . . . There was one condition, however; the preaching had to be done on Saturday. On Sundays business was too good to be interfered with by religion. In some places liquor and religion mixed readily. The bar not only remained open, but served as pulpit. Men serenely drank and played poker while listening to the sermon, and the preacher himself unblushingly called for a shot of rye whenever his throat got dry. [16]

One story of a wake held in an early day Montana saloon shows how some men needed no encouragement to drink while tending to the sacred. The story, told by pioneer Henry Bose, begins with the death of Irishman Micky at Last Chance Gulch. Micky made his friends promise to bury him in consecrated ground, with a priest attending. Bose explains that the nearest priest was in Deer Lodge, so a group of men made a coffin and formed a large procession for Deer Lodge, headed up by a wagon carrying the body. But they found some "ground sluice" near the Pioneer bar, which meant, of course, that they needed to have a drink, and after a few drinks they decided Micky should have a proper Irish wake: "We had some real good singing and drinking all night. The boys all got pretty tired, so we made our beds on the floor around the coffin . . ."

The next day they set out again for Deer Lodge, but when they arrived, there was no coffin in the wagon and one man remembered horses rearing at a river crossing:

We all went to Deer Lodge and had a meeting in Pete Valiton's brewery. The next morning [we] started out from Deer Lodge in the wagon. . . . [A]fter a long search we found the coffin in the creek bed where it rolled. And there was poor Micky standing on his head. We had an awful time getting the water out of the coffin, but we brought the body up to Deer Lodge and buried it reverently with proper ceremonies. [17]

MINORITIES AND WOMEN

Chinese and American Indians were rarely welcome in the early day saloon and little more will be said here about the racism that ran at the core of this white, male bastion other than that.

The presence of women also was rare in the early years. Some saloons actually kept them out, but usually not for long.

As the early day camps began to grow, women, the "soiled doves" as well as the adventurers like Calamity Jane or Dodge's proprietress Kitty, were welcomed by a population hungry for the wiles—and no doubt tempering influence—of the opposite sex. From the early days women ran houses of prostitution in Montana, often situated upstairs from a saloon. The Montana Legislature passed legislation in 1907 outlawing women from entering saloons, likely aimed at discouraging prostitution, but many bars simply added a side room and entrance for women, with bells used to summon the barkeeps. The last houses of prostitution were not closed in Montana until the mid-1970s.

Dixon found in her archaeological study evidence of women's presence in boomtown saloons from the very early days. Forensic testing that included DNA recovery showed that the stem of a tobacco pipe recovered in the dig was used by a woman of African-American descent who frequented the Boston Saloon in Virginia City, Nevada, a saloon with an African-American clientele.

Dixon uses this evidence to suggest a different view of the typical saloon patron.

This provides an incentive for rethinking the stereotype of the western saloon as white and dominated by males. . . . It also circles back to the topic of vices, drawing attention away from women's participation as servers of men's vices and to the idea of women as active participants in indulgences of their own. Even a most respectable woman will engage in such activities if she likes them—and many respectable women did. [18]

Erdoes notes in *Saloons of the Old West* that many western women were treated with more respect and given more freedom than their eastern counterparts because of the role they played in the settling of the territory. He notes that: "Women competed with men as bullwhackers, mail carriers, saloon and hotel keepers, bartenders, hunters, gamblers, prospectors, bandits, cattle rustlers, and owners of businesses." Their engagement allowed them to forge an earlier emancipation than they would have had had they stayed in the East:

Western women played a larger and more central role than their more sheltered eastern sisters. The frontierswoman could shoot straight if she had to, could ride a horse, drive an ox team, set a broken bone, make soap, grow her own food, make her children's clothing, slaughter a pig, and raise a family without many of the tools and gadgets normally used in a city household. . . . [19]

Of course, it also was women who led the crusade against alcohol.

THE FALLING SHADOW OF PROHIBITION

By the turn of the century the Montana saloon had become an institution. Over four decades it had grown increasingly lively, diverse, decorative, and perhaps a trifle arrogant. It had a reputation.

The camps also had grown. Tenuous settlements had become bustling trade centers. Town halls, hotels, mercantiles, and churches had stripped the saloon of many of the roles it had once enjoyed. Montana towns finally were achieving some sort of permanence, and with that came the yearnings of a good part of the population to turn a camp into a community.

That longing for stability and community was to play straight into the hands of the Temperance Movement. The movement was gaining momentum in the East and making tentative inroads in the West. But many Montanans probably still agreed with an assessment made by Charlie Russell, who in his own estimation spent half his waking hours in Montana saloons:

"Whiskey has been blamed for lots it didn't do. It's a bravemaker. All men know it. If you want to know a man, get him drunk and he'll tip his hand. If I like a man when I'm sober, I kin hardly keep from kissing him

when I'm drunk. This goes both ways. If I don't like a man when I'm sober, I don't want him in the same town when I'm drunk." [20]

A news dispatch carried in the *Butte Evening News* in November 1906 cited Montana as "the only state 'Entirely Wet.'" The story credited Nevada and Idaho as competitors, but concluded that Montana was the only state where bars were open twenty-four hours a day.

The article may have sobered up a few Montanans. The next year was to see the passage of several city ordinances ordering the closure of saloons for a few hours every night. Several cities, including Helena, Missoula, and Bozeman, passed what were called early closing ordinances. Most of the town newspapers editorialized against the ordinances, and often they passed by slim margins. Helena had a particularly lively session, but those for a more stable community were the winners. They claimed they could make Helena the educational center of the Northwest—one of the most progressive cities in the state as well as the nation—if the ordinance passed. [21]

In 1917 and 1918, as more states ratified the Eighteenth Amendment to the Constitution, articles speculating on what the future might hold began to appear in newspapers. The longtime rivalry between the smelter city and the richest hill on earth surfaced in one newspaper article. The *Anaconda Standard* ran a story on approaching Prohibition on January 14, 1917. The headline was vindictive: "When the Saloon Door No Longer Swings To And Fro; When Beer No More Shall Flow, And The Whiskey Bottle Vanishes And All Other Wet Goods of Commerce Disappear And Butte Wakes Up To Find Herself Dry As A Bone."

Predictably, in this working man's town, the lead of the story was the number of jobs that would be lost to Prohibition: "The total number of persons affected by the move, as near as can be figured from families of saloon workers, will be about 1,400."

Two years later, with the amendment ratified, Byron E. Cooney, one of several talented Butte journalists of his age, wrote a lengthy tribute to Butte saloons. Years later, another Butte journalist was to write an epic poem to pre-Prohibition Butte bars. Through the 108 stanzas of "The Saloons of Old Time Butte," Bill Burke named and described some 233 bars.

Cooney's article took the reader on an entertaining, emotional tour of several classic Butte joints. Many of the old-time bartenders were closing their doors never to open them again. But a few were to remain open through more than thirteen dry years.

Walker's in Butte was one of the survivors. Mr. Parker, the proprietor of Walker's, then a popular working man's bar, claimed his near-beers were selling well and he planned to stay open. "Near-beer served ice cold is a palatable and healthful drink," Cooney quoted Parker. [22]

Walker's and countless old-time saloons like it were to become the speakeasies, the Hire's root beer outlets, the milk-shake fountains, and the card rooms. It was at this time that many of the old-time saloons began stocking sporting goods and magazines. Prohibition did not kill the saloon. It just gave it one more role.

MONTANA AND PROHIBITION

Of course, Montana was never truly dry. The state legislature had ratified the Eighteenth Amendment to the Constitution in a special session in 1918, but in 1926 Montanans voted to repeal all state prohibition laws, leaving enforcement to the federal government. Having voted against it in a state ballot, Montanans seemed to prefer to believe Prohibition did not pertain to them. Butte was especially hard to contain. Erdoes writes:

> . . . [A] number of saloons kept their swinging doors open from beginning to end of the noble experiment. Washington sent out federal agents at regular intervals to enforce Prohibition in Butte and other parts of Montana. Most of them were bribed, some were never seen again. [23]

The popular theory that people drank more during Prohibition than before or after clearly holds water here. An article in a Butte newspaper during the period claimed five hundred speakeasies existed. Traffic was also heavy in border towns. Before Prohibition, Canadians crossed the border for American whiskey. Now the shoe was on the other foot. Montana News Association articles later were to describe a moonshiner's relay from Canada, through Havre, to Denver and Salt Lake, and shorter runs between Canada and Montana:

> In every hotel along the High Line there are groups of men garbed like Arctic explorers ready to make a dash for the line. Their talk is not of the defeat of the Non-Partisan League, or the drop in the price of wheat, in both of which subjects there might be some local interest, but rather of the run they have made that day. . . .

Moonshine stills sprang up across the state, but there was an easier way to secure one's Mornin's Mornin'. Alcohol was sold under various guises across the drug store counter.

Moonshining and bootlegging were the subject of many articles that were to appear in Montana during Prohibition and after. An article in a Butte newspaper listed several alibis given by moonshiners: as a stimulant for a baby; for money to feed children; a preparation for cleaning clothes; as a liniment and for bathing.

Other articles warned the customer to be wary of the "poteen." One cautioned that one in every ten bootleggers was caught. A Missoula legislator made the mistake of claiming to know of one bootlegging operation in 1919. The state's Attorney General subpoenaed

☞ Stools waiting for seats in Butte's M&M. Open since the nineteenth century, the M&M managed to survive more than a decade of Prohibition.

him, but he claimed constitutional rights and was not made to testify.

But all that was to pass. The Noble Experiment was to be viewed as a miserable failure by 1932, and in 1933 the saloon doors were to swing open again. Only beer was to be legal for the first eight months. Moonshine whiskey had been available through much of Prohibition, but beer had been more difficult to obtain. Their breweries closed during Prohibition, Montanans awaited the arrival of beer from eastern breweries with great anticipation. One account notes that beer was legal April 7, 1933, but it could not be shipped before that day. It usually took four days to transport beer from the Minnesota brewery that was to supply Montana, but the writer noted, "somehow it got to Montana two days after it became legal . . . Hundreds walked or drove to the railroad stations; the supply was exhausted within a few hours." [24]

But a look at Butte newspapers in early April tells another story. Several bars in Butte advertised a stock of eastern beers in the April 7 and April 8 editions. Walker's had remained open twenty-four hours every day through Prohibition. An advertisement in the Butte *Daily Post* claimed it had in stock the only draught beer in Montana. Walker's had survived more than thirteen years of near-beer. It seemed only right.

THE MONTANA BAR TODAY

Today, many years removed from Prohibition, the Montana bar has retained its function as the social sanctuary of the West: a place to buy supplies, fill up the gas tank, eat dinner, or end a long night of good-timing. A place where lifelong plans and promises are made, and just as quickly broken. A place to cry in your beer over life's inherent injustice—before you laugh with abandonment in the glow of one too many beers. A place to dance when the jukebox's western twang becomes too melancholy or too exuberant for a body's rhythm to ignore. More than anything a place to gather. Montana—as beautiful and accommodating as she can be—is still a lonely place, remote, a land of seemingly endless proportion that dwarfs people, frightens them, pulls them to one another. The town bar has always been the gathering place for the people who populated the harsh plains, the ominous mountains. Sometimes there was no town, but stuck out alone and brave, a refuge to the people tucked in the land's folds, was the Montana bar.

1

LIVINGSTON AND THE PARADISE VALLEY

In the Paradise Valley it's still not unusual to ride a horse to a bar. Just ask Phil, who's hanging out at the Two Bit Saloon in Gardiner the Monday morning we stop in. I consider this and contemplate the possibilities. Riding a horse is kind of like riding a bike, with the added advantage that the horse has the power; you don't have to pedal. But you do have to stay on.

Phil is a bit of an expert on this topic as he has been cited numerous times, he says, for Riding While Intoxicated. He was a horse trainer at the Chico Hot Springs stables for seventeen years, he tells me, and when he wanted to go to the Old Saloon in Emigrant, some three or four miles away, he'd ride a horse so he wouldn't have to worry if he drank too much while there.

He was stopped four different times, says Phil, and each time he told the arresting officer that his horse was the designated driver. "Horses don't drink," he tells me. I agree that's probably true, alcohol anyway. That was in the days of a sheriff who people keep referring to as a jerk as opposed to the good sheriff, who came later. The judge threw out the charge and told the sheriff to leave Phil alone. That's the story, anyway. And it's a pretty good one. If you saw Phil, dressed in his worn duster coat, missing a few teeth, with gnarled but lithe hands, you'd probably believe it, too.

I don't think it's simplifying things to say people go to bars to tell stories. What was striking about our trip to Livingston and the Paradise Valley, our first foray into the bar search, is how stories became entwined between people in several bars in different towns. We first learn of Sally, Livingston's former madam, at the Whiskey Creek Saloon.

At the Old Saloon in Emigrant we meet Burt Swainson, who knew Sally. Burt's grandparents homesteaded in the Paradise Valley and his parents were ranchers, but Burt took another path. Flight fascinated him, so he became a pilot. He flew a lot within the Paradise Valley and out of Yellowstone National Park, and one of his regular customers was Sally.

He said Sally always said a prayer before takeoff. He often would fly Sally's prostitutes to other towns in the region; this was a common practice—to rotate the girls. "I never hauled any more respectable people in my life," Burt says. "I've hauled dead people, live people, scumbags, and politicians, but the prostitutes were the classiest people. They dressed well—very well. And they were great tippers."

The Whiskey Creek Saloon
110 NORTH MAIN, LIVINGSTON

To get this project started, we decided to take a three-day weekend trip from our home in Missoula to one of our favorite areas, the Paradise Valley. There's Kelly, my partner; our dog Bailey, an old but spry American Eskimo; and me. It's one of those bright and brittle days in March, when the sun is making promises of spring it likely won't be able to keep. We believe it anyway. The Clark Fork tumbles brown with icy water, Butte lies spread out on a metallic slope, Whitehall sleeps under a downy blanket, the Gallatin Valley opens wide, as usual claiming bragging rights to Old West vistas—what could have been. In a moment we are there.

As we pull into Livingston and park on Main Street, I note a colorful bar front across the street, the Whiskey Creek Saloon. I know I didn't include it in my first book, but we agree it's worth looking at this time around.

Inside Kelly and I find a long straight shot of a room—about fourteen feet across, close to fifty feet in length—a handsome back bar, ceiling fans and chandeliers, a pressed-tin ceiling, poker table in the back. There are probably about thirty patrons at three-thirty in the afternoon and an almost equal division of railroad hats, cowboy hats, and fishing caps.

We take a seat at a table across from the bar where two forty-somethings are tying one on. They are in a hilarious state and it becomes infectious. The woman has conjured up a reality peopled with Keebler elves (something to do with the stature of another friend, a woman who stops by occasionally). The man is playing a sort of straight man to this silliness. Soon, we're pulled into their world and are laughing almost as much as they are. As often happens in a Montana bar, we are strangers being taken in by strangers. I consider this a good omen, remembering a similar experience in West Glacier that inspired my first search.

As we talk a little with the man (it's almost impossible to get the woman out of the Keebler elf story), we learn he had left the Mint Bar earlier in the afternoon because he thought he might have to "kick some ass." This would have been difficult, given that the man has had back surgery recently and walks with difficulty with a cane. The man is African American and there had been

☞ **The Whiskey Creek Saloon is one of many legendary bars in Livingston.**

a racial slur by another patron of the bar, so he came to the Whiskey Creek. He tells us he was the victim of a hate crime in the Mint not long after he moved to Livingston years before. The man who assaulted him ended up in prison for several years, and we're happy to hear that. I ask him what the best bar in Livingston is, and he says it's the Mint. I'm amazed. "Why do you still like that bar?" I ask. "Why would you go back there?"

"Cause this is America," he crows with determined chutzpah. Indeed.

A few minutes later a woman who looks to be in her eighties arrives, pushing a walker, a man of similar age behind her. She's greeted with a hug by the hilarious woman of the Keebler elf story and toots a horn on her walker, bringing greetings from the bartenders and other people in the bar. She moves back to the poker machines and converts her walker to a chair. Every once in a while she toots her horn—either to announce a win or call for another drink.

The next morning I learn that the Whiskey Creek has been around since 1902. It was the Old Faithful for many years. Sally bought it in 1974 when she was forced to close her house of prostitution. There was another owner, starting in the late 1980s until the early part of this century, when the bar was bought by an out-of-state architect who fell in love with the building.

I notice other things this Sunday morning that I had missed while attending to the Keebler elf scenario. A sign with the phone number of the local taxi holds a prominent position over the bar, near a sign that says PACKAGE LIQUOR TO GO. Complimentary coffee is available at all hours at a buffet table. Outside, a sign of a changing Livingston—an artsy metal-sculpted bike rack.

Murray Bar
201 WEST PARK, LIVINGSTON

The Murray Bar allows dogs and I like that. Bailey is immediately hit on by Oscar and Roy, the bartender's dogs. It's a little like an encounter between an inner-city gang and a newcomer. Or maybe it just seems that way to me as they bound up, barking. But Bailey takes it in course and soon is one of the gang. Dogs are easy that way.

We talk to bartender Nicole, a ski bum from Minnesota who took a job with a bank on coming to Montana but then quickly switched to bartending. At the Murray she makes more money, has time to ski, and can bring her dogs to work—a no-brainer.

The Murray has an impressive U-shaped bar, an upraised area for bands, a good-size dance floor, a pool table, and a great collection of bar flies—photos of regulars and other notable people framed, along with their favorite fishing flies. The Murray Hotel is listed on the National Historic Register, as are many buildings in Livingston, and its bar is a classic community gathering spot.

It's a saloon that lives up to Jimmy Buffett's "Livingston Saturday Night"—indeed it could have inspired it. I've been in the Murray on a couple of wild Saturday nights, and I have to admit the memory of the wheezy, animated sort of evening I had years ago when a band composed of local baby boomers had rocked the place had been in my mind on the trip over. After all, it's pretty easy to pull oneself up a flight of stairs to a room in the Murray Hotel after a night of dancing and overindulging. Alas, it was not to be. They're having music on Friday nights these days, so we missed it.

The Sport

114 South Main Street, Livingston

I've enjoyed the Sport bar for many years, usually stopping there when in Livingston. Opened in 1909, it's been a mainstay of the town for a century. In my first book I noted that antiques buffs would enjoy a visit because of the original back bar and a miscellany of interesting stuff, including an ornate player piano, rusty old tools—a primitive cattle de-horner, cracking leather saddlebags—and "a collection of newspapers that scream out the main events of American history in half-page headlines." I noted then: "The walls are packed with authentic western relics—a thousand of them if the Sport's claims are accurate."

Well, about all of that is gone. The Sport, owned by a long list of entities over the years, has been cleaned up—or cleaned out, however you look at it. It seems most of the locals aren't impressed; hence the business this Saturday night is slow. We belly up to the bar and order bruschetta and wine, which is the kind of thing you order in this sort of place. The bartender tells us the new owner plans to keep this as a bar and the memorabilia is safe—it will be up again. He says the owner has acquired the building next door and will serve food on that side, and the Sport will remain a bar.

I'll check on that the next time I'm in town. I miss the memorabilia and the dust, and the sooner they get it back up the better, but I have to admit, it may be the best bruschetta I've ever tasted.

Later, I'll stop in at the Mint Bar, which was featured in the first book. I wrote then about it being a railroader's bar. I must admit I'm a little prejudiced this time because of the story I heard in the Whiskey Creek. It hasn't changed much, with its mural of a "ferocious Northern Pacific stretching the length of the long bar." The Livingston Bar and Grill, first owned by Livingston artist and publisher Russell Chatham, isn't open tonight. It seems to be between owners, so we're left out of the tasty food the Grill has become known for, but we find succulent fare across the street at the Murray and enough mischief to make the night interesting.

The Old Saloon

210 Railroad Lane, Emigrant

Kelly and I arrive at the Old Saloon around noon, skewered from a night in Livingston and ready for something to eat. The Old Saloon has a basic sandwich menu, which hasn't changed to any degree in decades. We order hamburgers and take in the bar, which, too, hasn't changed much in the thirty years since I first described it:

The saloon's oak back bar and matching liquor cabinets date from the bar's beginning. A large mirror back stretches the length of the bar. The matching plank is old enough to have a copper and brass sink. The oak wainscoting lining the room looks untouched. The rotund wood burner sitting in the middle of the room radiates a soothing warmth, the bar's only source of heat. Outside is the original wood-plank sidewalk and hitching post. Red flock wallpaper, a worn wood-plank floor, and assorted antiques contribute to the old saloon flavor. The building itself has stood alone, basically unchanged some eighty years, with the same full-windowed front opening to the Absarokas and formidable Emigrant Peak.

I check out the restrooms, which still have wood-carved signs: FILLIES and STUDS. Soon both Kelly and I are watching three men who take up the end of the short bar. One is Burt, the man who flew Sally and her prostitutes. The others are Ken and Mickey. They're having a Sunday-morning cup of coffee. I overhear one saying something about getting a friend a sex change because of all his problems with women. They laugh and joke among themselves, then turn to us, the newcomers. Soon I realize the guy they're talking about is sitting between them and he's getting as big a charge out of the whole deal as they are.

"I like women," says Mickey, dwarfed between six-foot Burt and sturdy outfitter Ken. The two laugh about his disastrous liaisons. Pretty soon we're pulled into a

THE OLD SALOON

The Old Saloon was built in 1902 by Emigrant settler Ab Armstrong. Gold was discovered in Emigrant Gulch in 1864 and was still a going concern at the turn of the century. Gold scales (still in the bar in 2008) weighed out a miner's gold, and the customer would be given credit until the gold could be properly assayed. In those days the Old Saloon had two card rooms. One poker game became famous in the area. A news clipping hanging on the wall tells how a man called Kickin' Horse George kept raising the stakes one night in 1910 until he had pocketed $10,000 in one game. The Old Saloon likes to remember such individual achievements.

weird scenario of how this sex-change operation just might occur. It's silly but, perhaps because there's a woman involved, stays shy of the tastelessness such a subject might illicit.

"I like women," Mickey repeats. "If I had a sex change, I'd be a lesbian." The five of us keep up the banter and conjectures; giggles at times turn to belly laughs. Other patrons, who come and go during this adventure, smile wanly at us. The bartender is tiring of the whole shebang.

We did not expect this when we dragged our butts out of Livingston. We've found some new friends.

Kelly engages Ken in his life as an outfitter and experiences he's had. Of course, the topic of trophy bucks comes up, and soon we're discussing the male/female divide concerning placing head mounts in the house. I note that I won't allow it and there's no real surprise there from the men, except maybe Ken, who spends a lot of time in the wilderness. Burt asks the bartender if she allows her husband to bring them in. A quick and firm "No" is the response. It could be a light bulb moment for Ken, a handsome middle-aged guy dressed like he walked out of an old cowboy movie. "Maybe that's why I don't have a wife," he says.

Burt tells me he's now retired and lives on the family ranch, which has been appraised at millions of dollars, but he isn't interested in selling. "It's for my kids and grandkids," he tells me. "They're not making any more land." He bemoans what we all know now: "Movie stars bought up our whole valley," noting that hunting and fishing have been badly affected. Before, the locals knew where to go to access land and did it with little commotion. The newcomers have locked the gates, Burt says.

Mickey leaves and then returns. Soon we're back to the sex-change scenario and the coffee turns to beer and, for some, shots. But we can't stay forever, and pacing oneself on these adventures is essential. We exchange phone numbers and then pull the guys out on the wood-planked sidewalk in front of the bar with the same old hitching posts that I wrote about nearly thirty years ago. Kelly takes a photo of the guys and then tells me to step into the frame for a couple. Later I see how I had ended the section on the bar in the first book: "The Old Saloon, happily, is as much a local's bar as a tourist draw. In fact, it's the kind of place where the two might engage in a 'meaningful' conversation." I'm not sure how meaningful our conversation was this time around, but it sure was fun.

The theme that emerges from this three-day trip is one of imagination. Maybe it's because it's March and possibilities always seem around the corner in the last month of a Montana winter. Maybe it's because contributing one-liners to a strange scenario is a game all can enjoy. Or maybe it's because you're so damned bored with snow and isolation at this point you'll do anything to conjure up a laugh.

Two Bit Saloon
HIGHWAY 89, GARDINER

I think of the tendency to frame old newspaper front pages when I'm in the Two Bit Saloon the next day.

They still have two front pages framed—one crying out the death of Charlie Russell and the other the passing of John F. Kennedy, putting the twentieth century in perspective.

We arrive near noon, hungry for breakfast after a late night at Chico Hot Springs. We wonder if we'll be able to find eggs and hash browns so late in the morning. Sure thing, says Pam, the bartender at the Two Bit. Today it's quite slow in Gardiner, but nowhere near closed down. You can feel the anticipation of another summer season, but that busyness is still just a dream, and Pam is not going to lose customers in late March just because they want breakfast instead of lunch.

We watch her fry up a tasty breakfast as she tells us the Two Bit has new owners. Broken pipes a winter or two ago resulted in the closing of the downstairs bar, which had been the site of raucous concerts over the years.

I can remember a night in the early 1980s when Hank Williams Jr. played a gig here. There hadn't been much promotion and there wasn't much of a crowd, but my friends and I were delighted to have so much dance floor, even if the band appeared a little disgruntled by the turnout. Later we had a wild time at Mammoth Hot Springs and then tried to plop down in our sleeping bags not far from the river only to be awoken in the night by rangers and ushered back to the parking lot. I still can see the image of my friends in front of me, sleeping bags draped over their shoulders, walking single file down the path, looking like the lost tribe banished from paradise.

This is where we meet Phil and hear his horse stories. But it's also where I note a younger man tucked away in the bar's side room working diligently on a laptop computer. Wireless Internet has come to the Paradise Valley, and you see signs heralding it as you drive.

We keep filling our coffee cups from a side table as we chat with Phil and Pam about training horses and old times. We're content on this drizzly day, all our needs met.

Red's Blue Goose Saloon
206 WEST PARK STREET, GARDINER

Perhaps fitting the name of the bar, the stories in the Blue Goose are about wildlife. Or it may have something to do with the location. The bar's large plate-glass windows open up to the North Entrance to Yellowstone Park. "It's the Serengeti out there," says bartender Bruce, with a head nod toward the windows.

We look and see a small herd of bison ambling west along the highway, some nearly under the stone entrance archway. Stop, I want to stay, go back. I know Montana's latest method for controlling bison leaving the park is to gather them up and ship them away for extermination. No one can like this, but state wildlife people, ranchers, and proponents of the bison have been squaring off now for years and the wildlife seem lost in the bickering. Bruce tells us several thousand bison have been trucked off this year alone. What a sad commentary. The wild icon of the West killed for trespassing. Another lost tribe.

The Blue Goose attracts the river-rafting, mountain-climbing types, tourists and locals alike, with its impressive selection of microbrews, a poolroom in back, and a big flat-screen TV. It has a clean, airy feel to it, an emptiness in March that no doubt is a sharp contrast to its July ambience.

Bruce tells us what occupies the locals in the six-month winter. Much of it centers on wildlife, which roam through Gardiner as if it were a Yellowstone Park suburb. There is one elk—tagged No. 6—that has been harassing the residents for a few years. Seems No. 6 just doesn't care for people and he'd like them out of his way as he grazes through Gardiner. He's run several people into their homes and held a group of women at bay as they tried to leave the Baptist church. But he is old and has a wonderful rack, so the locals, including Bruce, are always hoping he'll drop his rack in their yard. The rack is worth a bit of money—a couple of grand at least. This year No. 6 dropped his rack—in the yard of a friend of Bruce's, the second time he's bequeathed her his crown.

When we got home from our trip and downloaded photos, we saw the photo Kelly took of the bison leaving the park. Behind them, another herd we had not seen when he shot the photo: a large grouping of pronghorn antelope, wearing the same dun and soft brown colors of the early-spring grass. Some are looking our way with an enigmatic gaze. White markings on their heads and necks are all that give them away.

Chico Hot Springs
1 OLD CHICO ROAD, PRAY

I've been going to Chico Hot Springs most of my life. Just being in the lobby of the resort brings up memories, like the one of my brother getting in a fight with a guy after the bar closed and me running up and down the stairs, alternately trying to stop them and hiding myself upstairs in case they roused the management and things got really embarrassing. Then there was the time in the second-floor hallway where I witnessed a masseuse urging my mother to indulge in a massage. God knows she needed it with five kids and a husband away on political business, but she was a farm girl and suspicious and said no. Years later my parents celebrated their fiftieth wedding anniversary here. Then there was the millennium party with a group of friends, all of us bringing in the next century from a joyous spot in the pool as a Chico staff member did the countdown.

The bar brings on similar memories—of dancing and conversations and stories told by friends. My favorite: In the winter of 1995, Kelly put our puppy Sophie on a bar stool next to his and ordered a whiskey for himself "and a water for my dog"—and got it. The bar is part and parcel of this historic lodge, but it's also a hangout for locals—people who populate the Paradise Valley or drive down from Livingston—and they are the ones we talk with when we come here. There are bands on weekends, and it can get a little wild.

On this trip most of the bars have been pretty smoky, with people puffing heartily the last year before all public places in Montana are to be smoke-free. But the Chico bar serves food (as tasty as bar food gets), and neither dogs nor smoking are allowed today. I have to laugh at a sign on one wall: IF YOUR SMOKING, YOU BETTER BE ON FIRE. Usually misspelling and poor syntax on signs annoy me, but this one makes me laugh. I'm at Chico and, as usual, I'm relaxed.

2

BUTTE

It would not have occurred to me that I would meet the next president of the United States while on my bar search, but I got lucky. A few weeks after the Paradise Valley trip, I find myself with Kelly and my father, John Melcher, in Butte for the annual Mansfield-Metcalf dinner. We've just come from Missoula, where Barack Obama has addressed some ten thousand people at the Adams Center. Both he and Hillary Clinton will be speaking to a few thousand lucky ticket holders who are flocking to Butte for the occasion. We get into town early to secure our tickets and have a couple of hours to kill, so I say let's go to the M&M.

M&M Cigar Store
9 NORTH MAIN, BUTTE

The M&M has been around forever. In that eternity, it has harbored all brands of vice while keeping the lid on tight enough to still be considered "Butte's living room."

As such, it attracts a broad swath of Butte citizens and all their guests, which results in large crowds that in turn attract politicians. On St. Patrick's Day and other days of festivities, it can take an hour or more to make your way through the place.

A few steps in the door and we run into people we know and are soon having a great time catching up. I recognize Stevie, the shoe-shine guy. It's strange. I know his face from when I had lived in Butte nearly thirty years ago. We both have aged, have lived a good part of our lives, and here we are again.

He's wandering around looking for work among the animated crowd and isn't getting many takers. I keep nudging Kelly and Dad, telling them they should get a shine, but they're too engrossed in their conversations. I look down and realize I wore boots that could take a shine and stick my foot out as Stevie comes around again. I note a man in the back of the bar, an outsider by the looks of his sleek suit, tight haircut, and intent demeanor. He's spending a lot of time on his cell phone but his eyes roam the bar.

Our friends leave and we find other folks we know, order another round, and settle in. Then I hear from someone: "He's here." "Who?" I ask to anyone who might respond. "Obama" comes the answer. I can't quite believe it. I look and see a crowd at the front door and, above most of the heads, that unmistakable short-haired noggin and big ears, surrounded by granite-faced Secret Service men with ear-plant cords running down their necks. It's Obama alright, and he's coming into the bar.

The crowd is massing around him and the excitement is palpable, but Barack quickly calms everyone down. He takes time to talk with each person he encounters, smiling gamely for photo after photo. I alternately stand back and move up to see what is happening, brimming with glee, amazed at our luck, a die-hard supporter who has hit the jackpot in the M&M.

He eventually makes his way to where we're standing and I introduce my dad, a superdelegate to the convention who has just come out for Obama. He's easygoing and fun—out of his blue suit for the moment—a polartec jacket softening his look. There's a lightness to him that contrasts with the leaden ambience of the M&M. Dad does something silly like hold his arm in the air and yell "Butte, America for Obama." Obama laughs and we talk fly fishing a little. Barack lifts his left arm and does the 10 to 2 motion to show he's serious about a

remark he had made at a rally that morning about wanting to fly fish. He shakes my hand and gives me a little hug before he moves on. I'm over the moon and will be for a few days afterward.

Obama makes his way to the back of the bar, being sure to shake hands with the bartenders and the short-order cook, and a few minutes later I notice him reaching out to Stevie, who seems frightened by the attention. I learn later that Stevie had asked Barack if he could shine his shoes and Barack had declined but wanted to talk with him a little. Stevie was overcome with the attention and moved away from Obama, the only one in the bar likely to do so.

A month later, I'm back and able to take some time to reassess the bar I opened my first book with. I called it "the dirty old man of Butte bars, a tobacco-stained grandfather who is still revered and respected for what he was in more vital days, and now, if for no other reason, because he's still around."

Reading that, I realize living in Butte when I wrote the first book may have inured me to the fundamental importance of the M&M as an institution. It is probably the best-loved bar in Montana. People realized how much they loved the place when it closed for a few years at the beginning of this century. The world without the M&M? Come on, now.

It was never just about Butte. People from across the state would meet in the M&M, know they could stop in any time, day or night, and get a drink, a meal, maybe play a little poker. St. Paddy's Days were fun, but more than packed. It was the regular morning, noon, or night that most of us enjoyed. So when the doors that had never been locked before World War II were closed up tight, a little sigh went out over Whoville and Montana seemed diminished, a key part of our past lost. When the bar was reopened in 2006 it was appropriate that Montana's Governor Brian Schweitzer stood and threw back a shot at ten in the morning. The world would go on.

The front of the M&M is incongruous in Butte—shiny steel in rich folds, a set of heavy steel doors below a large, mint green sign with arrows blinking to the bar's entrance. Inside is a long oak bar; directly across stands the cafe's equally long counter. The only thing that seems to have changed about the art deco back bar is that the lighted yellow columns from thirty years ago are now green.

A few weeks after the Obama encounter, my friend Simone and I stop in for breakfast around noon. The food is good—with just the right amount of grease, as usual. I miss the gambling action in the back room, which was the common denominator in earlier years. It seems empty and sad today.

A young man comes in and mops the floor between the food counter and the bar. Soon I notice the man has opened the bar. I move from one side of the M&M to the other, the most common traffic pattern in the bar.

There I talk with Jamie Robinson, who is managing the bar and is a partner with owner Dan Klemann, who bought the bar in March 2008. I order a pint of a microbrew and ask him what the charge is. He says two bucks. I tell him what I'm up to and note that when I first wrote up the M&M a small draft was twenty-five cents and a boilermaker a dollar. A boilermaker with Jameson's whiskey (called a Sean O'Farrell in Butte) is $4.50 today. They call it a Happy Meal. In my first book I talked about the crowds the M&M drew: "The place was loaded—front to back—from morning through the night. Politicians running in the spring primary worked the crowd like they'd work a farmer's convention or a large church bazaar." I talked about how Charlie Bugni served corned beef and cabbage for a dollar a plate, complete with salad, mashed potatoes, and coffee. Jamie says Bugni could keep his drink prices low and serve corned beef and cabbage for a dollar a plate on St. Paddy's Day because he made so much on the gambling in the back room.

He tells me the idea is to get back to what the M&M was like in its heyday. And they're not just talking cosmetics. They're talking high-stakes gambling. Upstairs. Blackjack. Poker. Craps. Slot machines. Butte's legislative contingency had pushed to allow full-on gambling in a section of Butte in the previous Montana Legislature but had come up short. Montana doesn't allow Indian tribes to run casinos, so Butte, the town that was Las Vegas before Las Vegas, doesn't get to either.

The Butte delegation's legendary clout with the legislature may not be what it once was, but Dan and Jamie are betting on something else the city is known for—a dogged persistence. "You can't tell Butte it can't do something," Jamie explains.

They have long-term plans for restoring the upstairs to a gambling hall, and Jamie asks me if I'd like a tour. Are you kidding? I've been intrigued with the upstairs since I learned about its role as a speakeasy during Prohibition. The M&M never really stopped serving alcohol during those years; it just moved the exchange upstairs. For years after Prohibition it served as a gambling hall, and when they no longer could get away with the sort of gambling they had upstairs, they moved the poker tables downstairs and put in the keno game. Of course, there were always the local betting pools as well.

"Butte used to bet on anything—how much rain would fall in June, for instance," Jamie says, adding that the pot for that bet was $5,000. He says they're going to construct a Wall of Fame in the back room of the bar— photos of all the old M&M gamblers. Among them was Swede, known for saying "you kicka me, I kicka you" when someone upped the ante. Black Hat Ray, who played 678 straight days of poker, eating all his meals in the M&M; a sickness finally ended the streak. Chinaman Joe, known for saying "me get some sleepie" when he was winning and wanted to pull out. The Kid. The Rock. Schlitz Belly. They all had their handles.

Jamie lowers the stairway to the upstairs, and Simone and I gingerly follow him up the stairs into history. The rooms clearly were abandoned and not thought much about for years. Furnishings are spread around, covered by decades of dust. Jamie shows us a large blackboard—about three feet by six feet—with odds from the Dewey-Truman presidential election. Truman's

odds? 20,500 to 5,000. A few people made some big money that night.

There were all sorts of bets on that election, line after line penciled out in colored chalk on the old board. The odds were 100 even that Dewey would carry Wyoming and Colorado.

We walk into another room. There's a full kitchen, the massive stove looking almost new. The windows are pure, thin glass. The ceiling's about twenty feet up. Sunlight streaming in frames the dust in the air.

Jamie says he thinks the high rollers were allowed in the smaller front room. The door to it has a sliding peephole. The masses used the larger room in the back, where chandeliers still stem from the vaulted ceiling. We make our way around the abandoned furnishings. Spirits and dust cloud the air. I see the player side of a blackjack table looking sadly up from the floor and vow to return and play blackjack in the M&M before I die.

Jamie gives me a keno ball, No. 12, from the early days as a memento. Then he pulls a shot glass out of a dusty box. It's thin and slightly tapered, five inches tall. It's mine. What a day.

☞ The distinctive sign of the M&M, a bar many consider "Butte's living room."

"EVERYBODY WAS HERE"

Numbers and the rattle of keno balls echoed in the M&M throughout the day and into the night when I wrote the first book. Elderly women in stylish leisure suits—their faces heavily powdered, their lips apple red—sat on folding chairs in the back room and watched their keno cards. The M&M's plank was usually lined with old men, bent to the bar like old crows over a telephone wire. But the place has always drawn all kinds. A lunch hour at the M&M then might have found life insurance salesmen rubbing elbows with workers from the Berkeley Pit, Tony the Trader charming a legal secretary, a motorcycle bandit in deep conversation with an area rancher. The M&M probably always has been most interesting in the early morning hours after the bars have closed. One time I stopped in with friends about three in the morning and talked with a student of Chinese, who had been sitting for hours at the cafe counter, drinking coffee and translating an ancient fable.

"Everybody was here," bartender Mickey Flynn told me over a beer one afternoon thirty years ago. "All walks of life. It didn't make any difference. They never locked the doors. During the war [WW II] they put the closing hours on. We had to go get locks and keys made."

Helsinki Yacht Club

402 EAST BROADWAY, BUTTE

I have a fondness for the Helsinki that I can't explain. I think it's the randomness that I wrote about long ago. Surprise is a key element of anything very interesting, and I'm often surprised when I go to the Helsinki.

It's name is one surprise—Helsinki Yacht Club—dropping "Steambaths" from the name and adding "Yacht Club" in reference to the sprawling, contaminated water-filled Berkeley Pit lapping at Finntown's "shores." Years ago I lived in Butte and frequented the Helsinki and its steam baths. This is how I saw it then:

A crumbling East Broadway Street ambles from Butte's uptown east to what appears to be the end of the road—the Helsinki, standing alone, in direct defiance to the wall of mining waste across the street and the mile-wide open pit beyond. The Helsinki is the last holdout of Butte's once-thriving Finntown. In 1941 it was one of six bars on the block. A few upstanding Finntown residents got up a petition to rescind the Helsinki's (then the Corner Bar) license because there already were five saloons on the block and the Helsinki was a scant three hundred feet from a church. Lucky for today's Finntown, the petition didn't fly. The five other saloons have succumbed to the pit, and the Helsinki, although quite lively some days and nights, has the demeanor of a place marked for death—a nonchalance bathed in fatalism.

Most of the humor you find at the Helsinki stems from that dichotomy. Of course, St. Urho's Day is the main joke. Finns love a celebration, and after a half century or more of enduring the Butte Irish taking center stage with St. Patrick's Day, Erv Niemi, owner of the bar, declared March 16 St. Urho's Day in commemoration of the "saint" who drove the grasshoppers out of Finland's vineyards. This was sometime in the 1970s, and he'd lifted the idea from a custom that began in Minnesota in the 1950s when students at Bemidji State College conjured up St. Urho as an excuse for skipping class.

The Finns in Minnesota jumped on the chance to upstage the Irish and the governor made it a state holiday; today St. Urho's Day is an officially declared holiday in all fifty states. All sorts of weird customs have arisen, including wife-carrying contests and women dressing as grasshoppers.

Is this weird or what? It is confirmation, to me at least, that Finns are some of the strangest people on Earth. The same site notes Butte celebrates with singing, drinking, and dancing the schottische— "hopping as high as grasshoppers." Music is central to most of the celebrations. Finns do love their music, which seems to ground them a little.

Today I'm a little disoriented when I come in the door. They've moved the bar and the place is clean, almost airy—with an expanse of floor space open for dancing. It's clear the steam baths are history, and I find this depressing. When I lived in Butte, I'd come to the Helsinki with some friends. We'd bring our towels on a Sunday afternoon, have a short beer, pay a dollar fifty each, get the key, and find our way out onto the snowy street and down the crumbling steps to a crude room with a bench that might give us splinters if we weren't careful. Inside a flapping door we'd find the gas stove emanating a fierce heat. Tossing water on it, the room became a cocoon of warmth, moisture, and fuzzy shapes in the mist. It was good. When you left you felt like you had the backbone of a snake.

I have many other vague but happy memories of ending a night in those crude but effective hovels (built in 1915, about a quarter century after the building was erected as a boardinghouse). One was taking my two-year-old niece, stopping on a drive from Forsyth to Missoula. For years afterward, she'd ask when we were going to the "Sinki" again. Another one was deciding with a friend after many drinks in the Windbag Saloon in Helena, in celebration of a victory of a political campaign we'd been working on, to drive to Butte to take a steam at the Helsinki. This friend was from the East Coast and I truly believed he needed to experience the Helsinki. The steam didn't disappoint, but it did bring us back to earth enough to not attempt the drive back to Helena.

That is the kind of thing you're not supposed to do at my age. But I'd like to know it still would be possible.

Simone and I begin at a table a little away from the bar. I note the TERVETULOA (Welcome in Finnish) sign on the wall behind the bar and a fabulous black-and-white photograph of a miner next to an ore bin. Before long we're at the bar, chatting up bartender Linda. She explains that the steam baths have been boarded up—too much of a liability. It's only mildly comforting to know that the insurance industry can shoulder the blame for another assault on personal freedom.

A man turns around when he hears my voice. It's Dave Corbett, brother of friend and beloved Butte artist Bob "Oxo" Corbett, who passed away a few months previously. Dave's grief is still palpable, fed by the recent death of his mother. Above the bar is a tribute to Oxo and his "foundation," a formidable structure south of town with eighteen-inch concrete walls that stored ore during the reign of the Copper Kings.

No matter how long I've been gone, I always meet a friend or two in a Butte bar. This time I wish with all my might that I could be meeting Dave and his brother. People who knew Oxo—and they are legion—know what I'm talking about. But time moves on, with and

THE BUGLE PLAYER

One late night in the 1970s at the Helsinki the Wyokies were seated in their usual perch in the corner. It was a warm fall night and the front door was propped open. My friends and I heard a commotion outside. We looked toward the door in time to see an old man come in. The man's stomach leered out of sagging pants, but his carriage was upright and proud. At his mouth was an old bugle that he was blowing with the concentration of a Lawrence Welk soloist. The bugle looked Civil War vintage and the man wasn't much younger. He blew as he approached the bandstand, nearly falling over backward once when he took too much breath for a particular phrase. The surprising thing about it all was that the man was good. The Wyokies played their regular fare, paying little, if any, attention to their colleague's counterpoint. The bugle player jumped around the melody, jazzing, jamming. Had the man been twenty years younger, sober, and with a presentable trumpet, we would have been in for some Music.

without us. Even the Helsinki has changed. But it's still thumbing its nose at the yawning pit across the street.

The Met Tavern
1375 HARRISON AVENUE, BUTTE

The Met is a favorite for many Butte locals—a sports bar that caters to all types. Today there are two young couples playing shuffleboard. It's mid-afternoon on a Saturday but they're dressed for a night on the town, the young women in dresses that hug their thighs and end several inches above the knees. The knees sinew down to shiny black heels that match their compact handbags. We're talking three in the afternoon. One can't help but wonder what the night might bring. At the bar a couple in motorcycle leathers chats with an older man in polyester. Regulars wait for the start of the Kentucky Derby.

Bobby Pavlovich and Herb Alesick (Herb the Serb) were partners in the bar until the mid-1990s when Herb bought Bobby out. Years ago Bobby Pavlovich told me about the night Evel Knievel barhopped through Butte. According to stories of two bartenders who worked that night, Evel had talked of hosting a party for Butte to celebrate before the Idaho Falls jump. Typically compulsive, Evel decided tonight was the night. He called Muzz and Stan's Freeway Bar to say he was on his way. The party began there and was carried to the Acoma, the Met, and finally, the El Mar. Evel bought drinks all the way. The crowd went with him from place to place, often spilling onto the sidewalks outside the bars. Bobby said the Met was "jammed to the eyeballs." He estimated Evel spent about $1,500 in each bar—a cool six grand. Evel's idea of a Butte six-pack. Pavlovich, well-loved in Butte, died a few years ago.

REMEMBERING BUTTE BARS

Butte, of course, has many other great bars. My friend Simone and I stayed in a suite at the Finlen Hotel on our trip, living large. For dinner we crossed the street to the Acoma Lounge and settled into the rosy cocoon of this great Butte hideout. It has been remodeled and is quite stylish and sleek today, but the booths are still as welcoming, offering a comfortable intimacy within a swirl of activity. The Silver Dollar draws the evening crowd to its funky dive with quality musical bookings. Tech students still crowd the Vu Villa. Muzz and Stan's is still going strong, as is the Deluxe—and we're not even touching on the neighborhood bars. But a couple of the best bars Butte had to offer are no longer in existence.

(continued on page 20)

(continued from page 19)
Luigi's Fun House of Entertainment

Luigi claimed Neil Diamond wrote "A Beautiful Noise" about his bar. You'd be sitting at Luigi's on an ordinary night and there would be a lapse in conversation or in the bizarre interaction between Luigi and his customers and Luigi's eyebrows would jump, his malleable face taking on an excited-child expression. He'd point a long, straight arm to the jukebox where Diamond's song was blaring, and stutter in his excitement to get the words out. "See, listen here now. It's a beautiful noise—the pipes you know, the pipes. Neil Diamond wrote that song about this place. He was here one night."

"A Beautiful Noise" could have been written about Luigi's but it really doesn't matter. As diverse and creative as the Montana bar can be, there was no bar in the world like Luigi's.

I spent a good many nights in Luigi's in the 1970s and early 1980s and I'm proud to say I was on his Christmas card list. Luigi was a friend of mine and many, many people, and he will always be missed.

Luigi called his place a fun house of entertainment. Early in the evening it was like a visit to the circus or the theater, a trip into fantasy or back into childhood. When Luigi really got wound up, there was no better description for the place than a madhouse. The bar actually jumped, spinned, thumped, flashed, blinked, winked, groaned, and squealed with his creations: puppets of all shapes and sizes; snakes hanging from the ceiling; reptiles everywhere, some set up to routinely devour others; a monkey on a unicycle riding a tightrope; a hammer that dropped to conk an unsuspecting customer when someone else opened the door; a full-size mannequin that collapsed when someone walked by; business cards and signed photos of famed personalities layered on the walls; and a large goldfish Luigi trained to swim through a hoop and kiss him when he put his lips to the water; all tempered by circling colored lights that blinked with a quiet amusement of their own.

The main attraction, however, was the world's largest one-man band, Luigi and his dancing dolls, all of which jumped and gyrated to the carnival sound of Luigi on the accordion, the drums, a couple of horns, a cymbal, the water bottles, a xylophone, and any object he could get his hands, feet, or mouth to.

With the various instruments and Luigi's throaty voice as background, down from the ceiling came the spiders and snakes. Tiny creatures, perfectly formed. A spotlight went on the menagerie of reptiles and they'd dance to Luigi's insane beat, the spiders' legs throwing large shadows across the empty dance floor.

Later in the night Luigi would find a regular or an energetic newcomer to mobilize the crowd. It was time to play the pipes. The pipes were old, hollowed-out antennas in widely varying lengths. Luigi would get everyone in a circle and put the song on the jukebox.

People would get down on their hands and knees—middle-aged women, a pair of traveling salesmen, teenagers, a couple in their early thirties, elderly pals of Luigi—they'd be on their knees throwing pipes across the shiny linoleum at one another, creating their own beautiful noise.

As the night wore on, customers would likely be waiting for a drink. Luigi often would say, "No thanks, I got one" or "Yes, I'll be with you in a half hour." When someone would ask when Luigi was going to play, the answer usually was eight minutes. The truth was Luigi played only when the feeling moved him. But he played every night, six nights a week for decades. And every night he was *on*. When I asked him years ago if he tired of coming in every night and doing virtually the same thing, Luigi answered, "No. You know why? Cause people are beautiful."

Luigi's first establishment was located in the little Italy of Butte, called Meaderville, famous for its gambling, food, and uproarious nightlife. When asked how long it took him to move his thousands of objects, he said, "Oh boy, about a case of vodka."

I remember my first New Year's Eve at Luigi's. Every age group was represented. Luigi was wild with excitement as the clock ticked toward midnight. You would have thought it was his first New Year's. Old women danced together, one in a flowing gauze gown, a whimsical young girl's expression on her face. Luigi did the countdown and when he came to zero I thought the place would rise from the ground.

(continued on page 22)

(continued from page 21)
Charley's New Deal Bar

At eleven in the morning the long bar at Charley's New Deal was more populated than it often was in early evening. Pictures crowded the walls—pictures of football and baseball teams so old the uniforms seemed as strange as men's two-piece bathing suits. Pictures of Halloween parties Charley and Esther Judd threw for the children of Butte for thirty-some years, pictures of various Democratic presidents. Pictures thick on the old, yellow-green walls, like memorabilia from a hundred grandmothers' living rooms. A silver bust of a noble FDR looked over the melee from above the bar.

Years ago when I visited Charley's doing bar research, Esther, Charley's petite, solemnly gracious wife, was tending bar. When she left for lunch her youngest son, Mark, took over, exhibiting the family aptitude for bartending that had kept some regulars coming in for more than thirty years. And then Charley himself shuffled in, a heavy, gregarious figure, gnarled and wise from all those years behind the plank.

Charley spent a good part of his childhood in Butte, but he was on his way to Nevada in 1936 when he stopped in Butte to give his friend, Esther, a hand with her father's bar. He was going to Nevada to get in on the "gambling business." At that time Butte was the gambling spot in the West. Las Vegas was soon to siphon off Butte's Meaderville trade, but Butte was still the Big Time in the 1930s. It had every sin a man or woman might hope to indulge in. And it had jobs for everyone.

Charley and Esther began throwing Halloween parties for the kids of Butte in 1942. I stopped by during Halloween 1978. The bar was closed; no liquor was served. The place was bursting with kids of all sizes. Tables were stretched the length of the long room. Costumed children, most of them escorted by their parents or grandparents, walked through the line as adults scooped candy, apples, and popcorn into their sacks.

The Judds would get nearly one thousand kids through their doors on Halloween night. Following the 1979 party, the New Deal hosted the older kids of Butte, the twenty-five to thirty-five age bracket, in a wild, costumed revelry that had been announced only by word of mouth. The music was jazz/rock piano and drum. The dancing could best be described as spontaneous. Charley sat in a corner surveying the scene, his usual broad grin reduced to a ghost of a smile. Perhaps he was seeing the thirty-year-olds coming through the candy line twenty years before.

The New Deal was the kind of bar that took on different personalities through the day. In the morning and early afternoon the old regulars were there, and friends of the family would come to chat with whoever was behind the bar. At noon teenagers from Butte High descended on the bar, ordering cokes and potato chips. Night-shift men drank at the New Deal throughout the day, but when son Mike returned from Missoula in the 1970s to bartend, late night began to attract a young crowd.

Late nights at the New Deal in the mid-1970s and early 1980s often reminded me of the now-gone Eddy's Club in Missoula, where in the 1960s and early 1970s, a crowd of journalists, artists, would-be philosophers, college students, and hopeless degenerates shared tables in the blare of fluorescent lights under a remarkable photographic collection. The conversation and flow of ideas rarely seemed to slow.

Eddy's often was very dirty; quite raucous; foreign to people who didn't understand it. But it was a rarity—a bar for a bar's sake—where you almost always found an old friend or made a new one. A bar to talk in, spit on the floor in, read a magazine in, do as you pleased in. Without pretense or camouflage. If you liked Eddy's you felt as good there at two in the afternoon as at closing time.

The New Deal was like that. And more. It was a Butte bar. It reflected the dual character of the town: a harshness bordering on cruelty sometimes found in its people, so much of their town and their past lost to the ever growing gray-ugly pit; that fatalism bred of a company town; the extremity of the weather; the frustrating disappointment of years of economic decline—easily overcoming all that, the generosity, loyalty, and warmth of a people who had learned that friends and neighbors are more valuable than all the ore taken from what, after a hundred years of mining, was still called the richest hill on earth.

These days the New Deal, appropriately, serves as a community center for Butte's youth.

3

DILLON AND THE BIG HOLE

A few months into my 2008 bar crawl it becomes clear that Montana saloons have not changed to any degree in nearly thirty years. Even I am a little surprised by that after a trip into the Big Hole. The Moose has been tamed—slightly—and the Metlen still feels vaguely genteel. Two bars I covered before—the Wise River Club and the Wisdom Inn—have undergone slight revisions, improvements even, but not enough to really notice.

In fact, when a customer tells Chester, the 2008 owner of the Wise River Club, that he lived in the Big Hole but moved out in the seventies, Chester responds, "Nothing's changed."

Moose Bar
6 NORTH MAIN STREET, DILLON
I remember the Moose Bar in Dillon as one of the toughest bars I'd visited. If it's still tough in 2008, I'll know it because it's about two in the afternoon on a Sunday when Kelly, a couple of friends—Michelle and Lenny—and I make it our first stop on a trip into the Big Hole.

Sunday is free pool day at the Moose. The front pool table hosts a group of Mexicans, and we spend a little time watching them play. I'm fascinated by one, a compact whir of energy who is making difficult, sometimes seemingly impossible shots. Like his friends, this guy is dressed in jeans, a clean, pressed western shirt, and cowboy boots, but unlike the others, he wears a rosary around his neck. I've traveled in Mexico a bit, but I've never seen a guy with a rosary around his neck. Depending on your perspective, it might be helping his pool game.

While we're watching, several of the guys' friends come in. Those not shooting pool—eight or nine at any given time—sit under the mural on one side of the bar—the cartoon replica of a heavy night at the

Moose I wrote about in the earlier book. When a new one comes in, he often buys a round of drinks and then ceremoniously moves down the line under the mural, shaking hands with each of his comrades.

I try to strike up a conversation with the most recent addition as he waits for his drink round—a tall, dashing young man who clearly likes the ladies. My Spanish is about as good as his English, but I learn that the men come in February to work in farming and ranching operations and go home in October. I ask him if they like the Dillon area. He laughs and indicates if they liked it they'd stay from October to February. He does admit to liking Whitefish, where he worked last year. Grinning ear to ear, he says, "the Canadian ladies . . . nice."

I talk to the bartender, a young woman named Casey who moved out West two years prior with cowboys from Dillon who were working at a dude ranch near her hometown in upstate New York. They said, "It's time to go to Montana," and she and two girlfriends said, "Why not?" The three women have lasted two years and have no plans of leaving. Casey enjoys calling her parents and telling them what she's been up to. They're often amazed. "I've done some stuff that I would have never experienced in New York," she says. She cites fly fishing, branding cows, and skiing as a few of the activities, but I suspect there would be much juicier fare if I were not taking notes. Later, I think many Montanan parents would be frightened by the thought of their twenty-something tending bar at the Moose. For Casey's folks, it's just part of

THE WINO PIT

The Moose's wino pit, a sad, small dark room, was off to the side in the back thirty years ago when I first visited. The late afternoon I was there, an old man was taking a nap on the floor. Later, I was told, the room would take on its nighttime personality. The winos were quite the musicians, the thick, earthy, middle-aged woman behind the bar told me. "They buy a bottle or a few cases together and sit in there and do their visitin'. They play their guitars, fiddles. They're educated men who just got lost along the way, with losin' their families and stuff," she said. "The majority is sheepherders."

an unfolding coming-of-age adventure. Of course, they've never been to the Moose.

I ask her what happened to the wino pit I wrote about in the earlier book. Casey tells me the wino pit has been gone for a while, but she's heard stories about it. She says they used to sell the winos a bottle and lock them in so they wouldn't bother other bar patrons or go out into the streets in the cold. I ask her if the Moose is still considered a tough bar. She says it can get pretty wild, noting a man got into a broom closet the weekend prior and found a shovel and was pretending to shovel shit for a period of time one night, to the hilarious delight of other patrons. "They get crazy in here sometimes," says Casey. "If there's a good song playing, people will get up on the bar and dance. They'll buy a bottle and walk down the bar, pouring shots into peoples' mouths. You see some random stuff."

Does she enjoy tending bar? Definitely. "You get to meet a lot of people. I could never sit at a desk." A patron approaches us and shows us some of the photos in the bar and encourages us to check out the Metlen and Sandy's new back bar. We tell him the Metlen is next in line.

Metlen Hotel & Bar

5 SOUTH RAILROAD AVENUE, DILLON

We meet Sandy on the way into the hotel and she tells us some stories. She says her mother owned the Metlen for years and loved it, a love Sandy doesn't share. "I got it the hard way," she says. "I inherited it." Clearly, she was quite close to her mother, and she promised her before she died that she would never tend bar at the Metlen. Why is that, you say? According to Sandy, a tough-talking middle-aged liberal who was doing just fine in California, thank you, it stems from an altercation in her younger days.

Determined to help her mother with the operation, Sandy offered to tend bar one night. She started with the best of intentions, but she's never been a wallflower and people, well, they just tend to grate on her, especially the conservative Republicans that populate Dillon and the Big Hole. That night her mother appeared, dressed even more elegantly than usual, according to Sandy. A patron noted she looked like a two-bit hussy, or something along those lines. Sandy remembers jumping over the bar to grab the guy by his throat, her feet dangling in the ice chest under the bar. After extricating the man, Sandy's mother told her she was done for the night and every other night. "This is a business," she said. "You don't do things like that."

Inside I pass on a little of what I'd heard from Sandy to Mayo, the bartender. He concurs. "When Sandy comes in here, everyone else goes out." Sandy has the hotel up for sale and doesn't rent rooms anymore, but she's created an authentic old saloon in a far back room that's open Friday and Saturday nights. I imagine Sandy

☞ The Metlen's well-preserved back bar was originally in Bannack, Montana's first capital city.

having fun decorating the den with Metlen antiques. She could enjoy the ambience without the people.

This is how I described the Metlen years ago, and it still holds, as it has changed very little other than it's now more than a hundred years old:

The Metlen Hotel sits across the railroad tracks from Dillon's main street. A large, boxlike structure, it has a casual class. This summer evening the doors are flung wide open and a soft breeze is cooling the lobby and lounge. The walls are clean, shiny knotty pine. There are dark red furnishings and a healthy growth of plants. Some eighty years old, the Metlen is a railroader's hotel, but like Dillon and the area—Wisdom, Wise River—there is also a feel of the hunter, sportsman, cowboy, and sheepherder about the place. There's more knotty pine in the Dillon area than you'll find anywhere in Montana, and the Metlen's pine is primo. Hand-carved pine trim frames the oak back bar in the small, low-ceiling lounge. The oak cabinets below the bar are beautiful, built for immortality.

Back then, both the Moose and the Metlen had spittoons built into the bars' footrests. They're gone in both places in 2008; I'm to find them in few of the bars I visit this time around.

Mayo takes us all back to see what they tout as a World Famous Back Bar. Indeed, the back bar is among the prettiest I've seen—and it's in remarkably good shape. Like many back bars I've seen on this trip, it was originally in Bannack, Montana's first capital city. A brass plate identifies its origin—Phoenix Furniture Co., Eau Clair, Wisconsin.

We see a framed photo of J. C. Metlen, who built the hotel at the turn of the last century, originally as a railroad hotel. A nickel cash register, engraved Metlen National, still works. The walls hold snowshoes and skulls, pelts, and taxidermy. Stained windows let in a languid light this late afternoon in May. Our dog Bailey and Michelle and Lenny's dog Druid have accompanied us on this little venture—the Metlen is dog friendly. In fact, later it is going to seem like a little doggie park.

We get Mayo to snap some photos of the six of us at the bar. We're all quite content; the dogs may be the happiest. They're not used to getting free rein in a bar. But it's Sunday and technically this bar is closed. We go back through the massive, empty building, passing through the extensive card rooms—Mayo says on days of celebration there will be five poker tables going—back to the main bar that easily accommodates a large stage and dance floor in the back, pool tables in the front.

Michelle has won the dice roll and some other game and has gotten two free drinks. Being a Scotch lover and noting a high-quality Scotch behind the bar, she's on her third by now. "The odds of getting drunk in here are pretty good," says Mayo. Later, when I buy a round for Michelle and myself, I'm surprised that two drinks cost $10; that little minx is drinking eight-dollar Scotch. Kelly and Lenny are shooting pool and the dogs are chatting up a little shih tzu that's arrived and seems awfully

DILLON'S LABOR DAY WEEKEND

Dillon claims its rodeo over Labor Day weekend makes for the biggest weekend in Montana. If not on the money, they're close. A good part of southwestern Montana can be seen on the cow town's late-night Labor Day streets. When partying over the big weekend many years ago, we pushed through the crowd and into the Crystal. An old woman was pounding an out-of-tune piano and a crowd gathered around her was singing songs like "A Bicycle Built for Two," "The Sidewalks of New York," and "Don't Fence Me In." The small straight shot of a bar rocked with the piano player's boots thumping the floor to the simple, solid rhythm. One of the singers—about 250 pounds of rich rancher—spotted a friend coming in the door. Realizing his friend wouldn't be able to see him, the big guy climbed up on his knees on a small, circular table next to the piano. The crowd was wary. The man balanced and somehow stood up. The crowd gave a collective sigh of relief. The rancher had caught his friend's eye. He tipped his hat to him. The friend joined the party and the singing burst with more exuberance from the collective windpipe of so many happy people.

excited to get to know them. Every once in a while one of them trots behind the bar to get a drink from the water bowl Mayo provides.

I'm talking to Mayo, who is telling me how he blew out his knee and wrecked a good part of his body in a nasty accident while competing in motocross in California several years previous. Mayo is a tall, handsome man who wears a baseball cap backward and jersey shorts and lives in an apartment in the Metlen.

He was in a wheelchair for three years, had nine surgeries and five implants, and finally got a battery-operated neuro-stimulator that interrupts the pain signal so he can walk. He followed his mother, who is renovating a bed-and-breakfast, to Dillon. Mayo's proud of his teenage son, who stops by. "They're all I've got," he tells me in explanation for his existence. And when we leave, he holds out his hand for a shake. None of us want to go, but it's time. If we don't, we'll end up sleeping on the Metlen's floor.

We pile into our cars and head west into the Big Hole—to Elkhorn Hot Springs, where we find a well-chinked cabin, fireplace, beds, and hot mineral water in which to soak the night away.

The Antler Saloon and the Wisdom Inn
101 MAIN STREET, WISDOM

What has changed in thirty years at the Wisdom Inn is the name. It's now called the Antler Saloon, and its present owner, who alternately prepares a tasty pizza and plays cribbage with a regular, tells me she doesn't know anything about the Wisdom Inn. As far as she knows, it's always been the Antler, but a drawing from my old book confirms this is the bar. Ah well, it's definitely been cleaned up. In my earlier book, I described it as a "funky old building that new owners have coated with bark in an attempt to enhance its western appeal. Any attempts to impress the tourist are forever suspended inside. The place is more a cluttered, musty taxidermy than a bar." I went on to describe the dust, guns hanging from the ceiling, and a woman mannequin dressed in inmates' clothing propped behind a barred door with a sign that said, JAIL. I'm wondering why I ever included this bar the first time.

Kristie Held has kept a bit of the taxidermy as well as the local lore, but the place is quite pleasant and clean, with a split, varnished ponderosa pine providing a nice second bar across from the main one, along with shiny captain's chairs. There are plaques in a corner that detail a good part of Wisdom's history. And she obviously kept the best of the taxidermy; a snazzy Canada goose soars above the bar. Two young women traveling through stop in for pizza, and a local comes in for a take-out order. Kristie's pizzas are quite popular in this area, and they do smell good.

I note some bumper stickers that seem to epitomize the attitude in these parts: TO HELL WITH THE WOLVES; SAVE THE RANCHERS; MY PRESIDENT IS CHARLTON HESTON; and NO TIME LIKE SNOW TIME.

Wise River Club

There's a little more action at the Wise River Club, an outpost in a vast mountain-ringed high-plains valley that dwarfs all who pass through it. A sign above the bar warns THE BARTENDER IS A MEAN OLD BASTARD, but that couldn't be further from the truth. In fact, Chester is an affable bear of a man with a slightly strange sense of humor. He and his wife Loretta bought the bar in 1995, and he's been having fun with it ever since. One of his favorite things to do is start "Buck" singing when it's likely to surprise a customer. Buck is one of many mounted deer heads in the bar.

Today the bar is quiet. It's a cold Memorial Day and not many are about. "I overslept and missed the spring," says Chester.

Suddenly, we're awoken from imbibing our mid-day cocktails by a lively bunch that includes two or three octogenarians and a couple of spry middle-aged women, one with her husband and young daughter, a beautiful child of Asian descent named Emma. They order drinks, plug the jukebox with coins, and dance—the bunch of them. We learn they've come over from Three Forks. One of the women talks of growing up in the area. "All of our life lessons were learned here," she says, referring to the bar.

Chester asks Emma if she's seen Buck. She walks over to him and gives him a look. Suddenly, Buck opens his mouth and sings "Sweet Home Alabama." It's pretty funny. Of course, the girl is intrigued. The soundtrack is first class, complete with band banter. So Chester continues the repertoire with "Rawhide" and "On the Road Again." Finally Emma tires of Buck and pulls a relative back out on the dance floor.

Chester tells us one of his sons bought Buck for him—got him in some box store. Then he shows us nineteen sets of elk antlers attached to the ceiling and extending from the front of the bar to the end and around a corner. They were all from one elk that was kept across the street, he says, in some sort of game farm. The elk lived for twenty-three years.

Earlier I described the Wise River as "a classic old hunter's lodge, with a room in the back stocked with comfortable old couches, chairs, and a wood-burning stove." Today it's still a classic, but the side room is large and airy, with a large dance floor, shuffleboard, and an impressive river-rock fireplace. The wood-burning stove has been moved to the bar side, where it warms the backsides of patrons. Chester warms their front sides.

4

GREAT FALLS
AND THE HI-LINE

Great Falls has always been a good bar town. And, coming off five days on the Smith River, Kelly and I are ready for a little bar-stool sitting. The Club Cigar is definitely on our radar after we check in at the O'Haire Motor Inn. We've stayed at the O'Haire a few times since we heard of the Sip 'n Dip bar, a spot I couldn't believe I missed in the first book. Later, I'll finally make it to the City Bar, a haunt of an old family friend. But today we stroll down the four or five blocks from the inn to the Club Cigar.

The Club Cigar
208 CENTRAL AVENUE, GREAT FALLS

John Tovson was fairly new to the bar business when I interviewed him thirty years ago. Then I was mainly interested in talking with Lena Ford, who owned the bar, leasing it to Tovson. Lena was a legend in Great Falls.

She ran the Club Cigar, a rough and rowdy Indian and cowboy bar, for forty years; and she operated one of the town's main houses of prostitution. It was said she would "bankroll" a hoard of ranch hands who frequented the Club Cigar when they got off the range and into town. She'd take their checks and dole out the money, usually spent in her bar, cafe, and house, until there was none left. Then it was back to pushing cattle. Researching my first book, I was told by a few bartenders what time Lena would shuffle into the Club Cigar for her nightly cocktail; they said you could set your watch by her.

I ask bartender P.J. who the owner is today. She says John Tovson, and he'll be in at 5:30.

We've been enjoying the clean ambience of a bar that only vaguely resembles the Club Cigar of the 1970s. Then it was dark and musty with a hint of treachery in the air. Today ceiling fans create a nice flow of air and there is a breezy lightness to the place. History is

LENA FORD

I met Lena Ford years ago when researching the first book. Before we met, I was both intimidated and fascinated by the prospect of coming face to face with such a local legend. Here's how I described the encounter:

Lena is in her eighties, a strong, powerful figure yet. She stands about 5'7", her body thickening, but nowhere near fat, her hair a halfhearted red tint partially covering the gray.

She and her friends have settled at a table in the back. The bartender approaches her cautiously. He tells her there's a woman at the end of the bar who wants to talk to her about the Club Cigar. Lena shifts her weight onto her feet, stands, then shuffles purposefully—with even a bit of grace—down to where I'm sitting. She extends a hand as gnarled as a limb of an old eastern Montana cottonwood.

Lena is nothing if not gracious. Someone wants to meet her, by gosh, they can meet her, but they'd better understand she doesn't have a whole lot of time or patience. She is the sort of woman any person with sense would never impose upon. Having developed the persistence and impertinence necessary in a journalistic career, I was pulled up short with Lena. Questions stacked up in my mind, tried to push out my mouth, but Lena was there. And she didn't have a lot of time. She was with her friends—old friends—and they always crossed the street about ten and had dinner at Sambo's. She had come to oblige, to meet me, but beyond that I was on my own. All I could get out of Lena without stepping over that line she had so clearly drawn was that she had "taken care of everyone—all the cowhands." Her voice was that of a chain smoker. There was hard living in it, but no age. She extended her hand again—what a hand—smooth, worn skin stretched over arthritic fingers, fingers bent at a right angle on the last joint—a strong hand, with a hell of a grip yet.

displayed in snowshoes and a noose hanging from the twenty-foot dark-wood ceiling. A refrigerated case offers the bar's namesake smokes. There's a very old wooden Indian, along with full-size cutouts of John Wayne and Jack Dempsey and bordello wallpaper. The monolithic mahogany back bar looms over it all. Bob Dylan is wailing on an expensive sound system.

Just off five days on the river, Kelly and I haven't even taken time to shower. It's clear the bar is much cleaner than we are. But I'm having a Great Falls Select on tap (not the same recipe as the old stuff—but no doubt much better—a microbrew out of Fort Benton) and Kelly's having some sort of beer, and the Club Cigar is smoothing any edges built up over five days on the river. We crack peanuts, eat them, and throw the shells on the floor, as suggested by the bartender. It feels a little odd; it's something we'd never do on the river.

A look around tells me John has remade the bar. Like all good saloons, it represents the personality of its owner. There's plenty of fun sayings on the walls. Our favorites today are: BLESSED ARE THOSE WHO EXPECT NOTHING, FOR THEY WILL NEVER BE DISAPPOINTED; IT'S A GREAT LIFE IF YOU DON'T DWELL ON IT; and THERE WILL BE A $5 CHARGE FOR WHINING. All of them resonate from our time on the Smith.

Before long John appears, and he laughs as we meet again. He remembers my piece on the Club Cigar well. Some thirty years later he tells me what the passing time has been like. The eighties were tough, he says. He did everything, of course—bartend, swamp out the place, order supplies. But he made it through and the Club Cigar put his two kids through college. He comes in these days to visit with the regulars.

He will tell you that on the block where the Club Cigar stands, there were once twelve bars—the Star Cigar, the Senate, Iron Pine, Pension, the Mint, Burk's, the Keg and Barrel, Glenwood, Husmann's, the American Legion, the Brass Rail, and the Club Cigar. Today it's just the Club Cigar.

John's a gentleman who is quick to take the attention off him, providing history of other bars in town and giving me tips for other places to visit. He buys us a couple of beers. We talk a little about Lena's bankrolling of ranch hands and, wouldn't you know it, a regular comes in and asks John, "can you give me another promo," which I realize means he wants a push on his tab. John isn't particularly happy about it, but can't say no.

I ask him about the clientele. We can see it's mainly downtown professionals at 5:30 on a Wednesday evening. John quotes a regular, who says "at ten o'clock the lake turns over at the Club Cigar." That's when the younger crowd emerges from the darkness to claim its spot on top.

Sip 'n Dip
O'HAIRE MOTOR INN, CORNER OF 7TH AND 1ST AVENUE SOUTH, GREAT FALLS

Piano Pat's musical stylings twinkle, and her adaptations of favorites cavort gamely over the ivories in the Sip 'n Dip lounge. Melting into a booth nestled in a corner in

THE HI-LINE

Years ago I spent five days driving the eastern Hi-Line in search of notable saloons and pretty much came up empty. Before my trip I hadn't been able to identify many choice saloons in that vast stretch of land forming the northeastern corner of the state. I was confident once I was able to do a little firsthand research a whole new world of saloon life would open to me. But if there was a new world up there, my boat missed the shore.

A five-day loop through Malta and Glasgow, on to Wolf Point and Scobey and Plentywood, then down through Circle, Sidney, and Glendive did little to inspire my search. The locals couldn't name any bars of note. The old saloons had either been renovated beyond recognition or no longer existed. So, as I traveled through fifteen hundred miles in that eerie meditation of land and sky, I developed a theory.

The Hi-Line was settled by farmers—family men, for the most part—unlike the cowboys and rustlers to the south, the gold panners to the southwest, and the trappers in the northwest. The sodbusters, also known as honyockers, were more likely to put up a church than another saloon. The towns they built during the boom farming years of the early 1900s were left to the relentless drought wind of 1917–1919 that swept the state, carrying with it a mass exodus of bankrupt honyockers. If there were few saloons to begin with, you can be sure few survived the killing drought and more than a decade of Prohibition.

It is a little ironic that the nomadic cultures of the cowboy, the miner, and the trapper, as reflected in their saloons, would have more permanence than that of the honyocker. But it is easy to understand when one remembers the social importance of the saloon to the drifter in unsettled territory.

this eastern Montana anomaly, one has the feeling of removal that only a circus or a tiki bar can inspire. In front of me is a teardrop table. Beyond that, a bar and an eerie eminence of pool, where mermaids swirl on Friday and Saturday nights. Not far above my head a grass-mat ceiling. Colored lights blink. A barmaid serves a glowing drink in a goblet the size of a beach ball. I'm not sure where I am, but I like it. Pat is crooning, "We love this bar. Now it's our kind of place …" Oh yeah. I order some fish and chips, sticking with the general theme, and watch the regulars at the end of the bar give way to twenty-somethings. The woman bringing my food could be my daughter, but she calls me "hon."

I lean back, my head on the padded booth, and listen. Customers, young and old, love Pat. "Fly me to the moon . . ." She's been playing here for thirty years and shows no sign of slowing down. A few years ago she released a CD that is sold only at the Sip 'n Dip. Her jazzy renditions of favorites in a lived-in voice throw a net over the place, reducing us to one big haul. "Sweet Caroline . . ."

Many people would ask what a tiki bar is doing on the windy plains of Montana. One answer might be that tiki was hot in the sixties when the O'Haire Motor Inn was the biggest new thing in Great Falls. Hawaii had just been admitted to the union and Montana was as happy to welcome the tropical paradise as any state. "Don't it make my brown eyes blue …"

It's been more than forty years, but if it was a good idea then, it's a better one now. This is true retro and just weird enough to make a lot of folks happy, especially on weekend nights when the bar is crammed to the gills.

One person it entertained was Darryl Hannah, who was in the area shooting a film in 2002. The star of *Splash* donned the Sip 'n Dip's mermaid suit and made many other people happy. *Gentlemen's Quarterly* featured it as the lead of ten bars "worth flying to" in its April 2003 issue when writer Andrew Smith admitted to being led around by the nose by a strapping young river guide. He didn't seem to mind. It's that kind of place.

Nice work if you can get it: Live mermaids swim behind the bar at the Sip 'n Dip.

City Bar
709 CENTRAL AVENUE, GREAT FALLS

I'd meant to stop in the City Bar on my first trip to Great Falls and didn't have the time, but today I'm driving my father around the state as he puts in a pitch for Barack Obama to various small groups. From the outside, the City Bar doesn't look particularly noteworthy. A 1960ish brick front and CASINO printed on a bright yellow awning aren't likely to pull me in. But I've heard about the bar for years; it was the unofficial "office" of a good friend of my family, John Boland.

John was an accomplished insurance man, rabid Irishman and Democrat, husband to the lovely Marguerite, father of ten, deadpan raconteur, friend to legions, civic leader, and urban operator. When you were with John, you knew you were in for a good time and you held on.

So it's not surprising I find myself in the City today with my father and John's son Jerry, who took over his father's business and seems more like him every day. It's only a few weeks before the 2008 general election and we're talking politics. But then politics is what we always talk with the Bolands. Several of their friends stop by to say hi. And I'm learning that there's quite a bit of Great Falls history in the walls. The bar was opened in 1939 by Anna and Charlie Watson, the grandparents of the man who now runs it, Brad Watson. His father and uncle, Bob and Bill Watson, ran it for years (Bob died of a heart attack in 1986). Brad serves us our ales and hands me a menu that includes a lively history of the bar.

The City does have a lot of poker machines, but they're tucked in a back nook. An extensive menu of sandwiches, salads, and soups makes it a good choice for lunch Monday through Saturday. The place is shiny clean with a wood floor, pleasant lighting, and sturdy tables and captains' chairs. A massive Brunswick back bar, installed by the first generation of Watsons, is gleaming, its inset lights providing a circuslike glow.

We're sitting near a refurbished Radiant Estate woodstove circa 1880s that was first used as a coal burner in northeastern North Dakota. Several antiques dealers owned the stove, one providing an impressive refurbishing before the Watsons purchased it in 1976.

It's commanding and lustrous and certainly doesn't look 120 years old. In the winter, Jerry tells me, people vie for the table near the stove.

Jerry tells us his father's view of the City was that it was the "Silver City," a "classy joint," where all the best people in their fields—white collar and blue collar—met at the end of the day. I know he'd be happy to see us here today. No doubt, he'd insist on buying the drinks.

The Palace Bar
228 First Street, Havre

The Palace definitely hasn't changed in thirty years. The same soaring mahogany back bar reminiscent of the back bars in the Club Cigar in Great Falls and the New Atlas in Columbus. The same pressed-tin ceiling. The long bar and high ceilings give a sense of grand loneliness to the place. Massive, fading five-foot-by-eight-foot duotones of a grain harvester and the Northern Pacific pay homage to the area's history.

A sign notes two happy hours: 5:30 to 6:30 and 11 to midnight; $1.50 for beers and mixed drinks. There's a few people clustered at the end of the long bar. One man is fingering out the alphabet in sign language to another.

Jupe Compton, one of the owners I talked with for the first book, has just left when I come in around noon. I call him later and learn he owned the bar from 1974 to 1983. He bought it back in 1989 and has had it since. He missed the place in the six-year hiatus. "I had it for so long it was like I lost one of my kids," he says.

WARD'S STORIES

Ward Compton, who owned the Palace Bar for seventeen years before selling it to his son, Jupe, in the early 1970s, provided a great interview for the first book.

Ward was a pleasant, articulate man who looked like he could be a bank officer or a wealthy rancher. Years ago, he told me, "All I've ever done is follow a cow around or have a saloon." The handsome Native American sitting next to me added an amen: "That's what you call a Montanan."

"Everybody, regardless of who they are or what they do, should spend a little time bartending," Ward said. "You mingle with the bums, the people who are average, and the aristocrats—it's a hell of an experience. You meet a lot of people in all states of mind."

The Palace used to serve as a seasonal employment service for select customers. Farmers and ranchers would come here when they needed workers, Ward told me. Havre, with its freight connections and seasonal farm work, was on the migrant workers' route, and many of them made the Palace their first stop when they arrived in Havre. Jupe would keep their packs behind the bar while they looked around town.

When a farmer or rancher came in looking for help, Jupe or Ward would match employer with employee. Ward claimed many farmers and ranchers would rather hire a man out of a bar than a man who refrains from drink but relies on government or local assistance. "They think they can get a better quality man out of a bar," Ward said.

Ward had some good stories about gambling at the Palace. "We used to gamble when it was illegal," he told me. "The law was always pretty good if you kept it in reason. When the police got too tough I had a room in the basement. We had a poker game that had gone on for twenty hours. An old man—Martin Wolfe—finally dozed off to sleep at the table.

"Martin was a gambler and that was it—a good gambler. It's real dark down there in the basement—no windows or anything. We turned the lights off and then dealt the cards. It was pitch-black. Martin woke up when we were bidding and started feeling around. 'You guys gotta help me,' he said. We just kept on like we were playing. Martin got more upset. He really thought he was in trouble. We kept playing. 'By God, Ward,' he said. 'I'm not joshing. I'm plumb blind.'"

His father, Ward, who owned the bar before he did and talked with me before, died about six years ago at the age of ninety-one. I note that I enjoyed talking with his father last time I was there. "He was a great storyteller," Jupe says. "I miss him every day."

Jupe says they still have a daily poker game at the Palace, and the only clear change he's seen over the decades is that now the clientele leans more toward the younger set—college kids. And the place doesn't function as much as an employment center as it did before. Farmers and ranchers hire fewer people these days, he says, because their operations have become more machine-dependent. But when they need a hand, they still come to the Palace. Tourists usually comment on the back bar, Jupe says, saying it's sure seen a lot. He usually responds, "If it could talk I'd have to burn the darn thing down myself."

I wish I could spend more time in Havre, but not this time around. Later I learn from a friend who lives in Havre that the Golden Spike is her favorite watering hole, what she describes as a bar not unlike the one portrayed in the television series *Cheers*.

5

THE FLATHEAD VALLEY AND BEYOND

Tell me there's a better way to see the Flathead Valley than from the passenger seat of a convertible sports car on an eighty-degree day in late July and I'll try it. But for now I think I'll just settle back and enjoy the ride. This is the kind of day when you might believe all things are possible. Freedom is not beyond the curve. It's not a thought or a concept or even a yearning. It is the bend in the gray ribbon of road and we are there.

My skiing buddy Dianne and I are on a lark, but a lark with a mission. Our first task is to locate the bar in West Glacier that inspired my first book. We drive along the road leading to the park but can't identify the bar. I see a building that seems to bring a flash of recognition, so we fold ourselves out of the Miata and walk up the stairs to the Belton Chalet. I had written about the experience of strangers in West Glacier welcoming me into the fold on a cold spring evening. It's with a bit of trepidation I enter today. I'm a little afraid of what we might find. I still have a mental picture of that evening and my instinct is to protect it.

We walk into a beautifully restored 1930s bar room with a large restaurant to the side and rooms to rent upstairs. It's not the bar, although it is situated like I remember the bar.

Later I learn that the chalet was renovated in the late 1990s to bring it back to its former clean lines and rustic grace. For many years it had been neglected. Part of its history was that it was called the Tap Room and was considered a "hotspot of the Northwest" in the 1970s. So, indeed, it may have been the place. It's okay that its oak is so shiny, the place so orderly today—historically correct.

But I feel a little lost when we leave.

Dianne revs up the Miata and I toss any longings over my shoulder. Soon she will deliver me to the Blue Moon.

The Blue Moon Saloon

HIGHWAY 40 AND U.S. HIGHWAY 2, COLUMBIA FALLS

What can I say about the Blue Moon other than it's been a part of my inner image of escape for decades? The first time was in 1971 when Richard Nixon came to the valley to dedicate the Glacier Park International Airport. My father, a U.S. congressman, and my mother flew out with the Montana delegation. I was there with my sister Tes and brother-in-law Gene. We had considered the idea that the before-dawn departure from Missoula might just be worth the effort if we got to fly in helicopters over the area. Dad was a Democrat and didn't have much standing with the Nixon people, so when they told him he could ride in a helicopter but his kids couldn't, he said, "Let's get out of here." The five of us crammed into Tes's VW beetle and drove to the Blue Moon, where we sat in a dark booth in a corner, downed a couple of drinks apiece, and congratulated ourselves on a brilliant escape. It was around noon, one o'clock. For a nineteen-year-old, that was memorable. Fact is, my Dad still remembers it.

Today I find a red padded booth in a corner and sit in it. I think it was *the* booth.

I had written about the people who bought the bar a few years after that visit in my first book—accommodating and naturally charming Charlotte and Dick Sapa.

I'd been in a couple of times after that, most lately a few years ago when I noticed a display of taxidermy on one end of the bar. Then I thought the bears were grizzlies and assumed someone had bought the bar. It seemed what an outsider would do—get some great taxidermy and put it in as a tourist attraction. I learn later that I was wrong.

Today we amble into the bar in mid-afternoon. I'm tickled pink when Dianne notices a sign that talks about the thirty-fifth anniversary of Charlotte and Dick Sapa's union with the Blue Moon. Soon I will have a talk with people that I interviewed in the late 1970s. We're back to Montana time. Change comes slowly over decades and generations, with some people inexorably riding a wave of destiny, pulling others along with them.

The Sapas are as natural and accommodating today as they were then. They grew up in small towns in North Dakota and Minnesota, went on a blind date, got married, and had three kids before you could shake a stick at them. Dick was determined to move to Montana. Charlotte didn't want to. She loved her little house, her family close by, that she could walk across the Moorhead State College campus to visit her mother-in-law. But Dick wanted to hunt and fish and he bought the Blue Moon in 1973. He said he was going to take his kids. Charlotte couldn't stand that. "Why didn't you tell him he couldn't have them?" I ask. "I didn't know any better," she says. "I was dumb. When we came here it was nothing but gravel road. There was nothing here. We had a car, but no one else did. They all had rusted-up old pickup trucks with a gun rack and two guns on the rack. It was awful." They lived in an apartment adjacent to the bar, where they raised their kids. I'd be here bartending at night," Charlotte says. "I'd lock the doors to the apartment. We had a German shepherd for a babysitter."

HIDING SPOT

Every time I've been in the Blue Moon, I've felt it a choice hiding spot. It seems to exist outside the normal pattern of things, an archetypal good-time bar. When I visited thirty years ago, owners Dick and Charlotte Sapa lived in an apartment next to the bar with their three children. I drank a couple of beers with them. It soon became clear then that the Sapas believed in a close association with the community. The bar was their home; friends and neighbors, customers. Charlotte called it being friendly. She said they were rewarded many times over for any good they did.

One afternoon, Charlotte recalled, soon after they had bought the Blue Moon, a young man was bragging about the horse he had just acquired. He told Charlotte he wanted to bring the horse over to show it off. Charlotte said, fine. (She told me she didn't want to discourage business.) Sure enough, the guy went and got the horse and rode it into the bar. He ordered a ditch for himself and a gin and tonic for the horse. Horses are supposed to like gin, Charlotte explained. The horse did slurp a little of the drink, but Charlotte said "he spilled as much as he drank." Sloppy horse. Crude, too. On the way out he lifted his tail and . . . The Sapas argue over who cleaned up the mess. An hour later I was about to leave. A young man came in, a friend of Charlotte's. He told her he had the baby out in the car. Charlotte and I walked out to the car with the guy. As I pulled out of the parking lot Charlotte was cooing over the baby.

Turns out Montana elk, moose, and bears weren't big enough game for Dick. On the front side of the bar, in museum glass with proper lighting, stand two massive brown bears taken on Kodiak Island in Alaska, claws ripping the air, along with a polar bear from northern Ontario and a small herd of mountain goats. Very classy taxidermy. But, in this case, it's just Dick bringing his trophies into the house. Upstairs a whole range of wildlife packs several rooms. Dick and his son go to Alaska every year and return with more. When he's not doing that or running the Blue Moon, Dick is ranching or checking in on the rodeo they host behind the bar on summer nights. "He likes to stay busy," Charlotte tells me.

Charlotte laughs as she remembers our first encounter. She keeps talking about me coming in and ordering a "scoop." It takes a while before she tells me what a scoop is—a draft beer, my usual drink on the bar trail. She thought that a little unusual. I'm not sure why.

It's not long before Charlotte's telling me about the death of her second son, hit by a train coming home from baseball practice. It happened more than twenty years ago but it could have been yesterday. It's ground Charlotte needs to cover.

The town pulled together and built the Sapa-Johnsrud Memorial Field. Charlotte is still a major baseball supporter. She sits at her place at the end of the bar every night and greets people, taking money for the latest cause. Today she's crowing about her grandson playing in a tournament in Washington. But the old days are not far away.

"Used to be, I'd be in here bartending, training a barmaid and a bartender, dealing with the band. Now they've got a name for it—multitasking! When we bought the place it was lit by two hundred-watt bulbs. We'd mop up at night after closing the bar. It was dark in here and hard to clean."

Charlotte is at her post most afternoons and nights at the Blue Moon. She tells me some stories about mayhem and court cases they've been pulled into. As a bar owner, "you're responsible for everything that happens," she says. "They can hold you responsible for what anybody does in here." I look over the expanse of the Blue Moon and note, "I guess it's like your living room." "Exactly!" says Charlotte.

Before, I wrote about the length of the bar. One of the longest in the Northwest—"more than sixty feet if you straighten it out." Charlotte says she's added a couple of serving stations, so it's even longer. Dick originally wanted a bar because he could combine family with his musical career. I wrote that he played "a wild country western six nights a week" in my first book. In his mid-sixties, he still fills in for musicians. "He played bass last week when the bass player got sick," says Charlotte. "We can do all the jobs around here."

The Blue Moon is starting to rev to a fine hum when we leave at nine that evening. They have bands Wednesday through Sunday night and book names on other days when they're coming through town. The bar is full, life is good, friends are abundant. Thirty-five years.

The Bulldog Saloon

144 CENTRAL AVENUE, WHITEFISH

Sometimes there's nothing better than a surprise. And the Bulldog is that. Dianne had asked as we started our journey, "What about Whitefish?" Indeed, I said. I didn't do a bar in Whitefish last time, but we should stop and check out a couple. "The Bulldog's the one," she tells me and she's right. A step in the door and you know you're in a world unto itself. The walls and ceiling are black, providing a sharp relief to the hundreds of decoupage photos mounted on primal colors of wood and varnished to a glow. They vie for space on every surface. School pennants hang from black ceiling tiles. Good smells come from the kitchen at the front of the bar, and take-out orders are flowing out the door at four in the afternoon. A couple of groups from Canada are taking up tables, settling in like regulars.

I note a sign behind the bar: WHAT WOULD TONY SOPRANO DO? and want to know more about the owner of this pleasant menagerie.

Dianne ushers me back to the women's john. She points me into one of the stalls, which is covered with photos of nude men displaying their equipment—all done in the same varnished decoupage as the photos throughout. Wow. This place is wild, I tell her. Whoever owns it is quite the decorator. We laugh at a few tamer posters that bedeck the main part of the restroom: MEN ARE LIKE POWER TOOLS. THEY MAKE A LOT OF NOISE, BUT IT'S HARD TO GET THEM TO WORK and THE DIFFERENCE BETWEEN GENIUS AND STUPID IS GENIUS HAS LIMITS. There's also a collection of photos of

Halloween nights at the Bulldog over several years. I'm reminded of Charley's New Deal in Butte. We check out a few more photos in the main bar—many of them Whitefish sports teams, but bulldogs get a bit of attention as well as photos of people doing strange things, like three middle-aged women costumed as colon polyps.

Back at the bar I notice families coming in and wonder how they keep their daughters and sons out of the X-rated toilet stalls. No one seems to pay the least attention. We order some fries and another drink and ask the bartender who owns the place. "Buck May," she says. "He comes in every morning from nine to eleven and talks with his friends."

So we're back the next morning at nine and here is Buck—an extra-large barrel-chested man with his bulldog, Maude. What a pair. Both have strong, round bodies and slight overbites. I introduce myself and somehow he knows I'm a Grizzly because one of the first things he says is he played football for Montana State. "How'd you do?" I ask. "We beat the Grizzlies three times out of four," is the reply. Not bad, I say. "What position did you play, center?"

"No," he says. "Why do you think that? Because I'm big? . . . I was a fullback." Later, I think of him running—I wouldn't have wanted to get in his way. But Buck is the kind of big man who is light on his feet. And he definitely has an artistic side. I ask about all the decoupage.

"People like to give you their pictures," he tells me. So he takes them, waits until he has gathered a few, and cuts the wood for the mounting. The wood for each is individual—cut unevenly and at odd angles to accommodate each photo. "I make them uneven so you can't tell if they're crooked when I hang them," Buck says. Now there's a manly practicality. Then he sands and paints the wood, decoupages the photo unto the surface, and applies three coats of varnish. Of course, there's a lot of drying time in between the steps. "It takes a while," he says with some understatement.

There are literally hundreds, possibly thousands, of photos on the walls. I'm stunned when I realize the work that went into them. And Buck has taken them all down, cleaned them, reorganized them, and put them back up to create more room several times. "This last time is the last time I'm doing it," he says, but I'm not sure he means it.

"People come in and ask where their photos are," he says. "They're used to them being in one place." He especially enjoys the photos in the front, which are of young kids. Often they sign their names. He says they'll come in with their grandparents years later and show them their photo and the grandmother will say something like, "couldn't you write your name any better than that?"

I mention the stall in the restroom and Buck laughs. "The human body is a beautiful thing—especially when they're nineteen years old." Can't argue with that. I ask him about the families who come into the bar. He's concerned, quick to respond: "Didn't you see that sign at the front telling people not to use that one with kids?" Nope. Ah well, there definitely is a family feel to the place and no one was kicking when we were there.

Buck has owned the Bulldog since 1982. He wanted to make it a community bar and a sports bar, so he named it for the hometown team. Maude is his ninth bulldog. He tells me bulldogs only live six to eight years. He and his wife were both schoolteachers in Havre, but decided they'd never make any money teaching. So she started a business and he bought the Gallery Bar in Havre. Wasn't long before the Pastime bar in Whitefish was for sale and Buck went for it.

From the beginning he took Canadian dollars at par in the bar, and it's served him well. Today he says Canadians are loyal and don't complain about paying dollar for dollar at the Bulldog. His son and daughter-in-law run the food side of the bar, just as the Sapas' son and daughter-in-law operate the Blue Moon's adjacent restaurant and casino. And today the two younger generations are all in Washington for a little-league baseball tournament.

Several regulars come in while we're talking with Buck. He greets them all. "You got your voice back yet?" he asks an elderly gentleman, who responds with a smiling, hoarse "Yes." Buck explains to us the rounds of chemo the man went through. A few minutes later a woman comes in. "How's the knee?" Buck asks. It's clear that they're used to having Buck to themselves in the morning but don't put up too much of a kick as he talks with me.

It's not until a nine-year-old comes in with his grandpa that Buck is ready to tell me the interview is over. The kid is hot to go fishing and when we leave, Buck is deep in conversation with him.

Moose's Saloon

173 NORTH MAIN STREET, KALISPELL

The first time I described Moose's Saloon, I said walking into it was "like opening the door to an eighth-grade study hall." Not much has changed. Both times I drop by during the summer of 2008 the place is wild. The first time I'm with my friend Dianne and there's a high school reunion going on. We're lucky to find a booth, where we tuck ourselves away to imbibe a few glasses of wine and savor a pizza. The second time I visit, on a return trip to the Flathead later in the summer, I'm with Kelly. After a quiet ride up from Missoula, the heavenly union of Flathead Lake and Mission Mountains taking the edge off the week, we're a little shocked by the decibals and the spectacle of the place.

Although it's a classic family bar (an infant was visiting with her family that evening) it's about as loud and raucous a saloon as you're likely to find. Pitchers emanate from the open bar, patrons throw down schooners of beer as if they're thimbles of water, and waitresses scurry around with pizzas extending like appendages from their arms.

Peoples' names are carved into every available piece of wood. And there's a lot of wood in the Moose. Heavy wood booths and picnic tables create a den in a large area across from the rectangular bar, itself thick with people. A bison head gazes sadly down near the front entrance, a bear trap dangles from a wood beam, and naked ladies in gilded frames glow on the wall behind the bar. The roar of the crowd drums into the ceiling.

Every once in a while, a primitive holler or sudden shriek punctuates the loud collective drone. Somehow it occurs to me that this is the sort of melee that might end in a human sacrifice. It's Friday night at the Moose.

We order a pitcher and eventually grab a couple of seats at the bar. Scotty, the bar manager, says it's a slow night. "The recession, I guess," he says. "It'll probably pick up after the homecoming game." Mental note: Be gone by then.

Scotty has tended bar at the Moose for thirty years. Moose needed the roof of the bar cleared of snow in 1978 and Scotty had just arrived from his native Minnesota. Scotty said he'd do it, and pretty soon he was behind the bar. He sees my old book, which I usually bring along with me for reference. "That thing is old," he hollers to me over the din. I holler back, "that's why I'm redoing it." He's surprised that I'm the author. "We've got one of those around here somewhere," he says as he hands a beer to a patron, shouting "that'll be two dollars and twenty-five pennies," then wrings the crank on an ancient National cash register that remains permanently open and throws a couple of beer bottles several feet to land in a large bin under the end of the bar.

The next minute the tall, lanky barkeep is doing a Tom Cruise imitation, pushing beer bottles down the bar, flipping glasses in the air, doing a towel dance. He's as fluid as the stuff he's pouring. I tell him about interviewing Moose for the first book. He's been gone, what, five years now? I ask. Coming up on nine, Scotty says, and then names the exact date of Moose's death.

TWO HUNDRED POUNDS OF INTELLIGENCE
AND GOOD NATURE

Interviewing Moose years ago was an adventure. I described him then as "6'3" and 220 pounds, all of it intelligence and good nature." Moose was a defensive tackle for the University of Montana Grizzlies in his younger days. He was all set with teaching credentials in 1957 when his wife Shirley inherited the Corral Bar from her father.

They came to Kalispell, where they found the Corral—"four bare plywood walls, two fluorescent lights, no business, and a $10,000 mortgage." What followed is a fine case history in business success. Moose expanded the place twice. Besides the large rectangular bar, the saloon had an area the size of a large dance floor filled with booths and picnic tables, and absolutely packed with people. The three hours I was there I didn't see a letup in the flow of beer.

Moose talked to me as he washed pitchers. He said he'd been lucky—got some breaks, some good press. He pointed to a story about Evel Knievel that appeared in *Sports Illustrated*. Evel supposedly concocted the Idaho Falls jump while drinking in Moose's Saloon.

Drinking what he (apparently no one else) called Montana Marys (red beer), Evel told the writer of the article, Robert F. Jones, that he decided he could jump the Grand Canyon while studying a photo of it in Moose's. "The more I studied on it and the more Montana Marys I put back, the narrower that durned hole in the ground seem to get. People talk about the generation gap and the missile gap and the education gap, but I suddenly saw that the real gap was right out there in the heart of the Golden West. And I knew I could bridge the bastard."

As the night wore on, I realized the key to Moose's success had little to do with an article in *Sports Illustrated*. Everyone in the place seemed to know him, at least well enough to call out a greeting. Moose functioned as friend/confessor/beneficent curer of ills. As we talked about bars and the strange and funny incidents Moose had witnessed, he became concerned that I not overlook one aspect of what it was like to own a bar.

He told me about Jack McCarthy, who for years owned a bar in Kalispell. Jack cared about people, Moose said. He'd take stray dogs and find them a home. He fed birds. And he buried anyone who didn't have a family to bury them. "Jack was in the bar business all his life," Moose went on. "He was the epitome of what a bar owner should be. How many guys do you know who would bury people? You have to actually have an attachment, a feeling for the people. A bartender should give you what you came in for. Too many people just throw you a drink."

Moose was back washing pitchers. He told a few good stories about bars, most of them unprintable. One morning he came in and found footprints all over the bar plank. He asked the night bartender what had happened. The guy said, "Ah Moose, you shoulda been here," and then went on to describe the striptease.

Very little in his bar has changed. Moose's daughter, Wallace, runs the food side of the place and is the owner of the bar. Two other bartenders are working with Scotty tonight, and they've learned how to bob and weave in the small area behind the rectangular plank. We sit and watch, and it becomes clear that there's a reason for three bartenders on a Friday night. No one waits more than a couple of minutes for their drinks. These guys are selling a whole lot of wine and beer. And they are in constant motion, like fish in a small pond.

The pleasant Canadian sitting to my right tells me that it used to be that someone in your party had to drain a pitcher—on his or her own—before they'd let you sit in a booth. I'm asking a bartender about the end of the summer party someone just mentioned. He starts to tell me, but a patron approaches and tries to order. The guy can't decide what kind of beer he wants. The bartend indicates all the beer taps down the line. The guy still seems to need some help. "You interrupted my conversation for this?" the bartend snorts and then gives him a confrontational stare. The poor guy is a little discombobulated. He wasn't expecting New York–style sparring in the Moose. The bartender basically tells him what to have and pulls the pitcher. The cost is nine bucks. The guy gives him a twenty and tells him to keep the change.

The bartend tells me the Moose throws two parties a year—the end-of-summer party and a Thanksgiving turkey dinner. There's free beer for two hours. Later I ask Scotty how many people they get at the parties. "About four or five," is the reply. I take that to mean four or five hundred.

A few minutes later an elderly couple and two older men come in the bar. Scotty lets out a whoop and their drinks are on the bar before they've pulled up their stools. Those four will be there when we've given up the ghost. An hour later we see the beginning of the crowd trickling in from the high school homecoming game. Three middle-aged women enter and take seats opposite us on the other side of the bar. They're clearly friends but not at all the same type. One is quite pretty, dark and exotic, and is wearing a cocktail dress that shows a healthy cleavage; another looks prim and proper, buttoned up. The third is a little bit country. Next to them is a large woman who is dancing to her own music, her arms billowing like seaweed in the air above her. She stops suddenly and bends to give the man next to her a long, deep kiss. He's a little surprised, but soon he's into it, too.

It's Friday night at the Moose.

Packer's Roost
8640 U.S. Highway 2, Coram

Today it's approaching noon by the time we get on the road north to Polebridge, and Kelly has in mind a beer and a burger for lunch. I had thought of stopping at Packer's Roost on an earlier trip, but there hadn't been time. Today we pull up to the fading false front and wooden porch next to a row of vehicles that are probably, on average, early 1970s vintage. One rusted truck has a five-foot row of beer taps mounted across its front grill. Yupper.

Inside we're greeted with a strong whiff of Lysol and several regulars enjoying the beginning of their Saturday. We pull up stools at a table and order draft beers and burgers and take a few minutes to settle in. Two women, who could be mother and daughter if you went only by age, are chatting amicably at one end of the bar, a group of men at the other. We see heads of natives, trappers, and wolves carved into dark wood, dollar bills with names flaming across them in various colors of magic marker tacked to wood beams and rafters, and what looks to be perhaps a hundred or more mugs hanging from above the bar. After a few minutes of observation, I become aware of the sound track on the stereo. Classic blues. Oh, yeah. A very good sound system and an impressive collection of blues. Kelly says he likes the place. I concur. It's got all the makings of an honest bar.

Reggie, the cook, arrives and, in a most pleasant manner, delivers our burgers. He brings extra napkins, saying we're likely to need them as we'll probably get into the food up to our elbows. He's right. They are very good, possibly rivaling the burgers of the Mo Club in Missoula.

I check out the Mug Club. For $25 you get your name on a mug and the first draft beer free every day. This is only one of the many good deals at Packer's Roost. We eventually learn that there are successive happy hours here. We only figure this out when we get the bill. We've

had two beers each and the second for each of us is about half what the first one was, which itself is less than what you'd pay most places. Kelly wonders aloud about getting another one, hoping the cost just keeps decreasing. Ha.

He asks the barkeep and learns that happy hour runs from noon to one o'clock, again from two to three o'clock, and then again from four to five o'clock. This is unique in my travels. And actually a brilliant idea if you want to keep patrons from leaving.

The bar itself is quite large, rambling, and worn; a formidable double-front woodstove is your first sight upon entering. The beer-garden area behind the bar features terraced rock patios, a sheltered stage, a fire pit, and a variety of seating options. It's easily more appealing than the bar. And it's widely used. In the summer, musical events are held here up to three times a week. People hold benefits and wakes in the back. Next week I see there's going to be a hog roast and live music. Three times a year—Easter, Thanksgiving, and Christmas—the bar serves a holiday meal to up to a hundred local people.

I walk back into the kitchen area to talk some with Reggie. He tells me to check out a few other bars in the area. He mentions the South Fork Saloon in Martin City, where the idea of bar-stool skiing came to be. He said a friend had been sitting around saying he should go skiing—if he could just get off his bar stool. Soon the idea for Cabin Fever Days was hatched, and all kinds of methods were devised for "skiing" down Sugar Hill, one of them on a bar stool attached to skis. That was nearly thirty years ago, and the event has become legendary. Reggie says we should check out the sleigh on skis perched on top of Packer's Roost's front roof; he used to put fourteen or fifteen kids in it with him and see how fast he could get down the hill. "The more kids I could get in, the faster we'd go," he says.

We decide to stop at the Deer Lick on Central Avenue in Martin City, and there we talk with bartender Doobey, a sweet middle-aged woman who has lived in the area most of her life. From her I learn about the local bar culture. These are working-class bars, most of them spawned by the construction of the Hungry Horse Dam, and they all have their individual personalities.

The South Fork Saloon sits up the street from the Deer Lick. Above that is the Dam Town Bar. That's where the poker run starts for Cabin Fever Days. To play your hand, you need to stop at the South Fork, the Deer Lick, Packer's Roost, Stoners, and the Dew Drop Inn. The winner gets a percentage of the pot, and the rest is divvied up between the Head Start government program, the local fire department, and the Christmas Fund. In so many bars I've visited I've seen this kind of community generosity; several towns raise money with poker runs.

Doobey tells us Sugar Hill got its name because Mabel's Cat House was located at the top of it. "Men would say they were going up to get a little sugar." Doobey adds that Mabel was very well liked in the area: "She was a real sweetheart. She helped the community. She made food baskets for people in need and she made mittens for the kids."

Northern Lights Saloon
POLEBRIDGE

I'm always happy when I pull off the gravel road to the dirt road that leads to the red false front of the Polebridge Mercantile. But after a few minutes I realize I've lost my second muffler to the road. That's two mufflers we've owned that have succumbed to this road. Later I learn it's the whole damn exhaust system. Ah, well. We've made it up to this remote setting on an opportune night—the night of the Polebridge Prom. Walking into the Mercantile I see the poster announcing the prom, next to a sign that says DRESSES AVAILABLE FOR LADIES.

I'm intrigued. It seems like it's going to be a hot time in the old town tonight. I see it costs five bucks to go to the prom and appropriate attire is required, including corsages. No doubt the Northern Lights Saloon, the only place to eat or drink in a good forty miles, is going to be busy, and it's already 4:30 in the afternoon. So Kelly and I decide to give up on renting a cabin up the road and secure our seats at the miniature plank of one of my favorite holes in the wall.

Our first visit to the Northern Lights was about ten years ago, and we were charmed. From the outside, it doesn't look like much—an old log cabin, its chinking almost as wide as its logs—with a weathered NORTHERN LIGHTS centered across the front. Inside, I've always felt a warmth emanating from the varnished log walls, the timber-crafted tables and chairs, the miniature back bar built by F.S. Company, the piano crammed in one corner, and the propane lamps providing a golden light. Every time I've been here I've enjoyed the drinks, the often surprisingly good food, the sense that I'm far away from life as we know it. And I've always enjoyed the company—always strangers, usually irreverent, often goofy, invariably fun.

Tonight our bartender, Paul, is wearing the appropriate attire of an old-time barkeep—a bowler hat, an ascot tie, a shirt, and a vest. His arm hangs angled in the air as he pours me a Tangueray and tonic. All drinks come in old fruit jars. Kelly has some red wine. We sit back, choose our dinner entrees, and watch as locals come in, dressed to the nines. They order drinks to take to the outdoors back arena that tonight is doubling as a high school gymnasium. I realize this is an end-of-the-season bash, with locals who live here only in the summer and others who hunker down for the winter heralding the end of the tourists.

The waitress at the Northern Lights is wearing a yellow flounce of taffeta and lace (circa 1962) that nearly reaches the floor. She's feeling quite fetching. Other locals arrive with all sorts of get-ups. (The next morning I talk with the cute twenty-something working in the Merc who is telling another young woman where to return her prom dress. It turns out that Northern Lights owner Heather supplies a wealth of prom dresses for women of the area or anyone passing through. "There's all kinds of dresses and sizes," she says. "It's amazing." Most of them are circa 1950–1962.)

There's a lot of high heels tonight, although one woman on the older side of the baby boom is wearing a formal fifties-ish dress along with sandals and socks. One very stylish woman is wearing a mid-length black cocktail dress that would work in a Manhattan watering hole and stylish heels. She's carrying a violin case—no doubt part of the music for tonight. I note a sign on the wall: THIS BUSINESS IS SUPPORTED BY PEOPLE FROM ALL WALKS OF LIFE.

We inhale the lime-marinated walleye pike and bison tenderloin with morel mushrooms. Kelly loves the potatoes and begs for more. I tell Paul I liked how he poured the T n T so much, I'll have another. It's convenient sitting at the bar, and Paul is taking a liking to us. Meanwhile, other people aren't faring so well.

Travelers always seem to arrive at the low hewn door of the Northern Lights with that expectant air, knowing they're going to have to wait in this tiny establishment powered only by generators and propane but glad to have made it to the only watering hole within miles. If they don't understand there's likely a wait entailed when they arrive, they soon get the picture. Polebridge has stubbornly held to the past, refusing to do its part to pave the road leading to it, eschewing electricity as a potential door opener to development, and generally disdaining tourists who aren't willing to take the place on its own terms.

But still they come.

This time it's a couple in their sixties, obviously feeling a little frisky, proud of themselves for having made it to Polebridge. The man orders a couple beers and asks Paul if it's worth driving the mile between Polebridge and the west entrance to Glacier Park—if there's anything spectacular they might miss. Paul is taken aback, not quite understanding. "It's Glacier Park," he says. The woman tries to explain: "Will we see any animals?" Paul still isn't sure how to respond. "No, they try to stay away from us," he says. "They're not going to be coming up on the road."

He has a difficult time keeping his frustration in check until they're gone. "Is there anything spectacular?" he repeats. "It's Glacier Park, for Christ sake." A group of middle-aged women, apparently back from a day of hiking, are becoming increasingly agitated. All they want are draft beers. Paul says they're out of Moose Drool, but they have Kokanne. They don't want that. He has a small keg of Slow Elk he's trying to open, but he keeps getting called away for other things. One woman comes to the bar and announces, "We're going to be patient." But the others aren't with her, it seems. Soon they're leaving, only to come back in and try one more time. Paul really doesn't seem to care. They give up for good the second time.

Kelly goes to check on our dog Bailey, who is waiting this out in the car. A few minutes later he's motioning to me from the door. I join him to watch a group of promgoers playing volleyball. What stays in my mind is the vision of a woman in her seventies wearing a coral bell-shaped formal that reaches to her ankles, her eyes intent on the volleyball, her arms seemingly frozen in position, getting ready to return a lob.

We ask Paul where he's from. Michigan, he says, adding he's going to Austin for the winter. Will he come back to work at the Northern Lights? Absolutely, he says.

A tall, lanky man has come in and he's beating out an intricate rhythm on his thigh with a couple of spoons. He's quite good, and I ask if he's going to play with the band tonight. "Maybe later," he says. "They're doing accordion music now."

We leave soon after, giving up our seats to others, and find a place near a boat launch to pitch our tent. The rain that had been threatening waits until about one in the morning, so the Polebridge revelers are safe, as are we. Next time, we're going to come up earlier. I'll get a dress and we'll go to the ball, I think as the rain takes me into a deep sleep.

Dirty Shame Saloon

29453 Yaak River Road, Troy

I guess someone had to do it. Someone bought the Dirty Shame and gave it a good cleaning. More than that, they cleaned up its lifestyle—so much so that many locals won't step foot in it anymore. I heard a little about this before the trip, but I know I need to check it out myself. What I learn is that the Dirty Shame died a typically raucous death and has been reborn as a law-abiding establishment that is really more coffeehouse than bar. Sacrilege!

☞ The Dirty Shame, for years one of Montana's most rough-and-tumble bars, is now owned by a stockbroker from Maryland.

The someone who bought the bar is Gloria, a sweet, smiling nondrinker who is explaining it all to me this Sunday afternoon. Memories from my last trip to the Dirty Shame are battling the reality of today. So many of the bars I've visited haven't changed to any degree. The Dirty Shame might as well be attached to a Barnes & Noble in Missoula. The rugged, packed outpost of yore that I stumbled into years ago is empty of people today, the ceiling and floors a handsome tongue-and-groove pine, a wireless computer beckoning from a shiny wood counter. The exterior false front and the deer-rack door handle are about all that seem familiar.

Gloria bought the place a few years ago. She says she had to do something with the ceiling. It was sagging in the middle. And then there were the bullet holes in one door and across the backside of the bar room. Gloria knew the previous owners, Willie and Rick, who were notorious for their fights in the bar. When they split, Rick somehow got the bar and Willie got the cabins out back.

Gloria and her husband had owned the Yaak River Lodge down the way and decided to buy the Dirty Shame from Rick and let their daughter and son-in-law run the place. But it turned out the kids weren't interested. Perhaps they weren't tough enough for the challenge. But Gloria is. Don't let that soft Maryland accent confuse you. She was a stockbroker for twenty years and she's not new to the Yaak.

And Gloria loves to cook. She's hoping to have some culinary students in to train with her next summer.

Culinary students at the Dirty Shame. Take a while to let it sink in.

We're a little late for the Sunday brunch, but some tasty-looking food is still in the warmers. It's after one in the afternoon, we've driven over from Polebridge with a blown muffler, and we're hungry. Gloria bustles around, scrambling up some fresh eggs. I order a Bloody Mary and it takes a while to get it. Kelly would like a beer but can't get a word in edgewise, so he eventually ambles away, crossing the street to drink in the Yaak River Tavern.

Gloria refers a few times to the place across the way, often throwing in a reference to how smoky it is. She comments how there's a "demand for food" in the Yaak that she fills. The place across the way has cold-cut sandwiches, she notes, but not much else.

It's hard not to like Gloria. It's clear she has taken some heat from locals and others who make the trek to this outpost, but she remains steadfast in her endeavor. And she's accumulating her own clientele, as witnessed by the four or five guest books filled with names and comments. A piano and setup for musicians brings that crowd. She also has book readings and draws many people who aren't close enough to the Yaak to be miffed about what happened to its legendary bar. And no doubt there are locals who are happy for the cleanup.

There's the wireless computer for anyone who wants to check their e-mail, and Gloria allows free long-distance within-country calls to anyone who wants to use the telephone. She says that helps with people who come and rent her cabins for $25 a night. "I had a girl in a few weeks

INFAMOUS

Thirty years ago I struck out by myself to visit the infamous Dirty Shame Saloon, a bar that catered to a sparse 150 people in about that many square miles of wild backroads. I'd been to the Yaak one time before, driving the relatively modern road up from Libby. This time I took the northern route through Eureka, over the Purcell range, some of the most beautifully untamed country in the state.

On the way out of Eureka, I was told how to get to the Yaak, and that I was crazy for going alone at night. The road is bad, they said, and there's no one to help if you break down. I was young then and decided to chance it.

A few miles out of town I took a wrong turn. It took me about an hour and a half to correct the error, and by that time I was on a hiking trail the map showed as a paved road, climbing a mountain pass. Two hours later I stumbled weak-kneed up to the Dirty Shame. The same wood-planked front porch, the same deer rack used as a door handle, the battered inside, the loggers, ranchers, recreationalists, Forest Service people—all using the bar like a third leg—a poker game in a corner, a huge wood-burner stove in another.

Back then the Dirty Shame had the fresh, sharp smell of smoky pine and the dank odor of dirt-laden beer-splashed floors, wild nights of revelry, and mornings of shared pain. Irascible, strong-willed, folksy, accommodating, the Dirty Shame was as honest a bar as you'd ever find.

It even came by its name honestly. Glenn Johnson, a compassionate, rotund logger/bartender, well respected in the Yaak and a patron of the Dirty Shame nearly two decades when I met him, told me the story. He said in the 1950s a man by the name of Kennedy noted that an air base was being established in the Yaak. He bought a beer license, hauled beer up from Libby, and set up business in a shack, grandly naming the place the Yaak River Lodge. The air force men manning a D.E.W. (Distant Early Warning) system had lived many places, but never in the Yaak. They drank at the Yaak River Lodge, but they didn't like it; most of them choked on the name. "It was a shack, and it was dirty," Glenn recalled. Eventually Kennedy got a liquor license, but the place didn't get any cleaner. The men from the base would come and drink because there was no place else within forty miles. They'd look around and then mumble to each other, "Now, isn't this a dirty shame?" The Yaak River Lodge never really had a chance.

Glenn told me the Dirty Shame was the result of seven shacks pushed together in one way or another. He'd helped with the redecorating over the years. There were many things that distinguished the Yaak and the Dirty Shame from most of Montana and the country, and some of these things still held true when I talked with Glenn. For instance, at that time everyone in the area burned wood. Electricity had come to the Yaak, but forget about natural gas. Locating, cutting, and storing wood for the winter consumed a good part of the summer and fall free time. The night I was in the Dirty Shame the widow of a man shot and killed two days before in an ugly incident was in the bar with several friends. When she left, Glenn told me they were planning a benefit dance for her and were going to "set her up with wood for the winter." The woman ran another bar in the area, and she burned about twenty-five cords of wood a year.

Glenn listed off several other benefits organized for people down on their luck. Besides benefits, the Dirty Shame was big on dances. On weekends they'd have local musicians play. "Hundreds and hundreds of dances," Glenn said. "No one stays home in the winter." Everyone would come to the Dirty Shame and make full use of the wood cut for the bar.

ago and she wanted to call her boyfriend all the time. She was pretty happy about having use of the phone."

Gloria is not immune to the history of the Dirty Shame. She kept what she could of the bar plank—chiseled with peoples' names—and the log bar stools. She'll show you the bullet holes and explain why the woodstove can't be used because of building codes. And she knows all the old stories. I mention the one about the guy who shot cattle and left them lying in the middle of the road outside the Dirty Shame. The story is that in the Yaak at the time, you had to fence cattle out of your yard, and this guy Jimmy claimed the cattle would come into his yard, stomp bicycle tires, and shake his trailer when they rubbed against it. He told people in the Dirty Shame one night, "I'm getting damned tired of those cows rubbing on my trailer and [me] walking home drunk every night through the shit . . ." He warned the rancher to keep the cattle out of his yard.

"Oh yeah," says Gloria, "the cow story. . . ."

She's got some stories on how the name came to be. One is that the fighter Joe Lewis came in and asked for a certain kind of Scotch. When they didn't have it, he called it a "dirty shame." Another one is that the mother-in-law of one of the early owners would sit in a corner of the bar and tell her son-in-law what a "dirty shame" it was that he bought the place. I stand by my story (see sidebar). I got it from a longtime regular thirty years ago.

I'm still trying to uncover what would make Gloria want to take on the Dirty Shame. Over the last four or five months she has had no backup. She's been open every day, doing it all. Her response: "I was a stockbroker for years. I've lived in Philadelphia, New York, and Washington, D.C. And this has been the most fun of anything I've done." She remembers how she came in to find the bar after Rick left. The ceiling was sagging, the place was worn and filthy, and Rick had taken everything but the pool table and the stove. It was May, and later Gloria learned the contractors shook their heads, saying the poor woman was in deep trouble. Gloria decided, "We have to be open for the Yaak Attack," which happens every year in mid-July. Somehow, she did it.

This late-September Sunday, Gloria is closing the bar and heading back to her husband in Maryland. She'll reopen in May. When I first heard this, I was amazed. How could the Dirty Shame close for the winter? That was before I realized the Yaak River Tavern had come to be. And the Yaak has changed. There are paved roads every way you look, a far cry from my first trip. And there's good food at Gloria's. You should see her kitchen.

The Dirty Shame is dead. Long live the Dirty Shame.

6

HELENA

The Helena area is steeped in history, and I find reminders of that in all the bars I visit over an August weekend. The Windbag was barely open when I wrote my first book and somehow I missed the York Bar, which I've been hearing about from a few friends. So this fine Thursday morning finds me with my brother John and niece Jill making the relatively quick trip from Helena to this outpost near Hauser Lake.

York Bar

7500 York Road, Helena

I immediately like the place. The false front and wood-plank porch appeal to me. Inside, we're greeted by a one-woman show, bartender Mary. She's getting drinks and frying burgers for ten or more people but still has time to greet every person who walks through the door. We pull up stools and order some burgers.

Many people assume the bar was named for York, the strong and gregarious manservant to Captain William Clark of the Corps of Discovery. Indeed, Lewis and Clark and their corps did come through this way, and it would seem likely the bar was named for him.

However, I later learn when talking to one of the bar's owners, Tina Moon, that York has been shortened. The original mining town was New York; another mining settlement across the road was called Brooklyn. So much for legend. But sometimes the truth can be almost as interesting.

The history of York is found in framed articles and photos in a dark side room with a commanding fireplace. Like many mining towns, New York, Montana, was established in the late 1800s. But its Golden Messenger Mine played out longer than most. The York School was built in 1899, the York Bridge in 1906. Brooklyn is long gone. The building housing the bar was first a post office and then a grocery store. The York Bar came into being in 1941.

The pine walls and low ceiling hint of hunting lodge. Dollar bills with peoples' names written on are tacked to walls and ceilings. People close to the bar usually stop in for a burger and a beverage and many, like us, drive the fifteen miles from Helena for that purpose.

"We're a destination bar," says Tina. "Last week I had people from England in here." The bar is also host to several celebrations throughout the year, including the York 38 mountain-bike race and York Fest, a fund-raiser for the local fire department and community center, in August (Tina: "We did sixty burgers an hour for that bike race"). The Duck Run is held in September (rubber duckies are let loose to race down Trout Creek, and the owner of the winning duck gets $500) and concludes with a huge feed and live band under a big tent. Sounds like fun to me.

Ting's

MAIN STREET, JEFFERSON CITY

Fortified with food and drink, we set off for Jefferson City to see if Ting's is still around. My main interest before was that it had served as a stage stop for the horse teams that ran from Fort Benton to Butte and from there to Virginia City. They used a twelve-horse team to transport merchandise, Brunswick back bars, eastern beer, and other goods brought to Fort Benton by steamboat. Every twelve miles, I wrote, there was "either a small town or a bar where the stage once stopped." And you can still see those towns today. Between Helena and Butte there's Jefferson City, Boulder, Basin, and Elk Park. Craig and Wolf Creek were obvious stops between Great Falls and Helena. And there was a stage route between Fort Benton and Billings, winding through the Musselshell Valley. The more you travel Montana, the more you note the tiny towns often found every twelve miles or so. Little Lavina, north of Billings, was once a stagecoach hub, with teams heading north to Lewistown, east to Roundup, and south to Billings.

Many of these outposts have vanished; others are barely holding on; and some have found other ways to thrive. Tings was a favorite stop and remained so long after the steamboats gave up on navigating the Big Muddy. When I visited thirty years ago, I had talked with Whale (pronounced Wally) Phelan, a grandson of one of the settlers of the Boulder Valley. He remembered his grandfather telling how he broke a new horse to pull for the stage run nearly every day. Today there's not much happening in Jefferson City. Ting's is about all that's left, and it's not looking too spry. We're not sure it's open until we pull on the door.

Inside we admire the Brunswick back bar with a wagon-wheel motif and order beverages. The bartender gets drinks ready for some locals as they open the door to the bar. That seems normal, but the feeling is that the bar is a ghost of itself. There's a stale stillness. All the fun is gone. A few minutes later we learn from the bartender that he and his wife are divorcing and have the bar up for sale. He's moving to Seattle. It's all very sad. Ting's is like the child in this divorce proceeding—left out and confused. Who knows if it will be bought? Who knows what will become of it?

Windbag Saloon
19 South Last Chance Gulch, Helena

We need cheering up, so we head to the Windbag for dinner. I usually stop in this establishment when I'm in Helena, partly because of its location on the gulch and partly because the food and drinks are always good.

The Windbag Saloon has seen a lot in the thirty years it's been around. The upstairs of the turn-of-the-century building has seen a lot more. It was Dorothy Josephine Baker's house of prostitution and before that Ida Levi's, both established businesses in Helena. In fact, Big Dorothy didn't get closed down until 1973, and then it was by order of a district judge in Rosebud County, Alfred Coate.

I'm reading this on yellowed newspaper articles framed and hanging in the back of the well-traveled bar and restaurant. I had never heard this story, at least the part where Al Coate played a role. He was a close friend of my family when I was growing up in Forsyth. It seems no one in Helena really wanted to put Dorothy out of business, so when a reforming county attorney was looking for a judge to rule on his motion he had to go about 300 miles to the east. They arrested and charged Dorothy in a clandestine raid.

Helena residents were indifferent to the idea if not hostile. Part of Big Dorothy's problem was Helena had attracted an urban renewal grant to help restore historic buildings in that part of Last Chance Gulch. The building now housing the Windbag was part of the St. Louis Block and was built in 1890. Dorothy had applied for some of the grant money to improve her building. One of the county employees at the time bemoaned Dorothy's indictment, saying, "She's the only person in this town interested in bringing her building up to code."

Dorothy never stood trial. A diabetic, she died in a Great Falls hospital not long after the indictment.

Randy Beckner, owner of the Windbag, says history lives on in the people who visit. "Every guy over the age of sixty-five or seventy used to deliver papers here, or groceries. Everyone knew it was here. They realized it was an established business. She took very good care of the women who worked for her. Anybody who delivered groceries said she tipped pretty well. She seemed to be a forward-looking woman in the sense that she knew how to run a business."

Downstairs housed a number of businesses over the years, including a burlesque hall, a movie picture theater, a bowling alley, and several drinking establishments. Four people opened the Windbag Saloon and Grill in 1978 and named it for the political animals known to be drawn to Helena.

Randy was in on the Windbag's early years, settling in Helena in 1980 after a few years as a ski and bike-riding bum. He started as a bartender and eventually became a partner and today is sole owner.

The owners' leanings were clearly Democratic, as a few black-and-white photos on the walls attest. My favorite is hung on the wall you pass as you go into the dining area—John F. Kennedy trying to restrain a boisterous Lyndon Johnson on an airplane stairwell. There's also a poster of a very young Mike Mansfield in one of his first campaigns and Jeannette Rankin being sworn in as the first woman elected to the U.S. Congress. George Washington is the only other Republican represented, and he wasn't even a Republican. (Some would argue Rankin wasn't either.) As you history buffs know, Washington didn't believe the country should have parties, but the Federalists claimed him as one of their own and eventually their ideas morphed into what we know as the Republican party today.

Early on, the Windbag was a Democratic hangout and it still is likely to draw politicians and supporters from that side of the aisle, but Randy says they get Republicans as well these days. "It wasn't beyond [former Governor] Judy Martz to come down. You just see a lot of people crossing the aisle these days. Everybody's pretty comfortable in here."

When they first opened, the nights when the legislature was in session were intense, Randy says. "We'd count the days until they would leave. They'd be out every night. Now it's not the rowdy out-every-night scene it used to be. Maybe they're staying more on task."

The Windbag's back bar and the stone walls of the dining area attest to the historical relevance of the place, along with the dark green walls and white wainscoting in the bar. But what really says nineteenth century to me is the entrance—with its high transom and weathered wood in a two-door entrance. Opening the door to the Windbag for me has always been like a step into the past, almost as intriguing as would be a step into the future.

The Rialto
52 NORTH MAIN, HELENA

I'm sitting in the Rialto on a quiet Friday afternoon and I can't get the bartender to talk to me. I don't know if this has ever happened. This kid really doesn't understand his role. But I'm enjoying the dark and quiet atmosphere on a hot summer afternoon in a bar that has hardly changed in thirty years. It's still a nice hiding spot in the center of town.

It's just me and two old friends a few stools down the bar, who are engaged in a lively conversation. And a bartender who refuses to talk to me. Occasionally service people deliver stuff. I note all the drink specials (flavored vodkas for $2—not bad), a bucket of PBRs for $10, and great deals on rum drinks for Thursday Ladies' Night.

Much of what I saw before remains: the art deco bar with its rounded forms; enclosed lighting that gives the room a red glow; wood trim dropped about a foot from the ceiling, something like a ribbon around the room, providing another illusion of being

FRONTIER TOWN

"Only God can make a tree, but I can whittle the hell out of 'em," John Quigley told me in what may be the best explanation for Frontier Town—a virtual forest of trees he whittled the hell out of. John built this replica of an early western town nearly single-handedly on a perch of rocky ground near the top of MacDonald Pass, taking most of a lifetime to make sure he got it right. Although Frontier Town is closed now and John has passed, his quest was unique and in some ways amazing.

Frontier Town was built of smooth yellow wood taken from the forest nearby, worked into whatever practical purpose the mind of John Quigley found for it, then varnished to a warm glow. When he didn't use wood, he used rock—massive stones and boulders, also found nearby. They formed the many fireplaces found in the bar, dining area, and lodge. The hallway to the dining room was a mosaic of stone worked into steps and walls, a medieval passage of cold rock that opened into an expansive dining area, built totally of uniform logs. John estimated that he used 525 tons of boulders and 25 miles of logs in construction.

As far as bars go, Frontier Town had a dandy. By 1953 two places had been used as bars. That year John expanded the lodge and built a new bar. He used a Douglas fir fifty feet long, about four feet in diameter. He found the tree in the woods near Frontier Town, cut it, and then split it clean down the middle. The bottom half became the bar plank and the top became the main ceiling support for the room. Standing back from the bar, one got the full effect—a fifty-foot tree sliced down the middle—one half holding up customers, the other holding up the room.

Hanging on one of the bar's log pillars was the framed photo of Quigley with a bear he killed in 1962. The hapless bruin—confused, hungry, or perhaps just dumb—had entered the building through the kitchen and found its way down to the bar around closing time

 The Rialto hasn't changed much in the past thirty years, but this mural of regular patrons is a nice addition.

one summer night. With his usual dramatic flair, John hung the photo above the spot where the bear died and mounted the bear nearby.

The room housing the bar was full of interesting antiques and oddities. One cabinet held gold pans and weights used by Quigley's grandfather, a pioneer Montana merchant. Spread throughout the place were quality antiques, some items the likes of which would be difficult to find in the state's historical museum.

Many of the articles were relics of Blackfoot City, a long-dead gold-mining town that once boasted five thousand people, a few miles from present-day Avon. John's grandfather, another John Quigley in a generational line of men of the same name that goes back to Ireland, settled in Blackfoot City in the 1880s.

Eventually he was the proprietor of the town's livery stable, a slaughterhouse, a store, and a bar. John kept one of his grandfather's ledgers. He told me the loans varied from a sack of beans to cash and always listed the nationality of the debtor—white, colored, Chinese, or Indian. Most of the debts were not repaid. Blackfoot gold did not pan out, and the town, like so many other mining settlements, was dead before the doctor diagnosed the illness.

John's father became heir to a good part of Blackfoot City when his father died. Eventually he tore down buildings for firewood, but the next John Quigley inherited something of his grandfather's spirit.

While his father was tearing down buildings, John was gathering as many of the old tools and household furnishings he could. And, as he watched the final deterioration of his grandfather's town, Quigley decided he would build another town, a showpiece of pioneer Montana, a town crafted from native material by his own hands, a town to hold the relics of a past receding as quickly as the weeds grew in Blackfoot City's main street.

In 1946 John bought what appeared to be a worthless piece of ground on rocky MacDonald Pass. He pitched a tent there and began to build, much to the skepticism of the locals. On a trip to Florida, John met Sue Whittier. They were married and returned to

Montana and a budding Frontier Town. Some thirty years and nine buildings later, John and Sue were still in construction.

In 1975 a fire nearly leveled the dining room. Much of the expansive room had been rebuilt the early spring day I stopped in years ago, but John didn't have a lot of time to talk. He was whittling on his latest project—a reclining bobcat—kept warm by a large wood-burning furnace, built, of course, by John himself.

Sue and I watched John whittle. He told me about the early days, when gold dust was used as exchange, weighed out on scales at the bar. In those days, a dishonest bartender would grow long fingernails, and when weighing out gold, he'd manage to get a quantity of dust under his nails. He'd walk off shift a good deal richer than when he came on. Another trick was to Vaseline one's hair and then coolly rub gold-dust-laden palms through the greasy locks.

We talked a little about the hard and lonely life of Montana pioneers. A visitor could feel the toil and sweat and years of work in a walk through Frontier Town. Yet there was a grace and easiness in the smooth, shining, functional wood, the fitted stonework, the clean smell of wood burning, the spontaneous hospitality of the Quigleys. "You made just about everything here, didn't you?" I asked John one more time. "Yeah," he said, "made everything here but money—and I'm working on that."

tucked in; the cozy half-moon booths seemingly built for smaller people.

I walk through the front area, where food is still served and you can still buy a good cigar. Not a lot has changed there, either, other than the fabulous wood refrigerated cigar cases are gone. There's still the 1930s lunch counter, custom-made by Weber Showcase Co. of Los Angeles. Burgers and other diner food are available. This is the real thing. You could feel like a ponytailed teenager in this place, cracking your bubble gum.

I see the gaming room has been moved to the side and a tiki bar added, along with a patio out back for smokers and overflow on busy nights. It's hard to imagine a busy night on such a slow afternoon, but it was slow when I visited before: "Heavy gilded frames hold old paintings above the heads of old men at the poker table. They are as much fixtures of the place as the wood trim. Panguigue is the game in the Rialto today." I take a gander at a mural of Rialto regulars that's been added since I've been here—not bad.

When I retake my seat at the bar, I'm still left to my own devices. Years ago I observed: "A solitary person nursing a draft beer is almost more than a good bartender can take." Uh-huh. When the bartender finally condescends to talk to me, I'm bored. I made a comparison before and it still stands: "In Helena, the Rialto comes closest to the community status the M&M Cigar Store enjoys in Butte. Butte's M&M is large, freewheeling, often decadent. Anything can happen in the M&M; virtually no one will be surprised. The Rialto is tight, stylistic, orderly, with a wholesome 1950ish air; its clients are easier to surprise."

Several people had told me the Blackfoot Brewery was about as popular a hangout in Helena as any. My editor Erin and her husband Ross arrange a tour of the new digs with one of the owners. They're finishing construction and plan to open in a month or so. It's beautiful, and from what I gather, a real community gathering spot. I vow to return.

7

THE MADISON RIVER VALLEY

Ruthie, Courtney, and I are gabbing gaily like women do on a lark as we head east from Missoula on a fine August morning. Our destination: Virginia City. My niece Ruthie was an infant when I was researching my first book. Back in the late 1970s her three-year-old sister Hannah accompanied me to Sleeping Child Hot Springs for research. Ruthie wants to make sure she's not left out this time, and she's bringing her best friend, Courtney, to take a long drink of Montana before she leaves for a job in Manhattan. Ruthie's hardly been out of Missoula in the two years she's taken to set up her yoga studio, so she's bubbling with excitement.

I'm happy to be with two young women who are slightly older than I was when I wrote the first book; it seems somehow fitting. And I'm to learn that they're game for the task as we pony our tushes up to some seven bars in less than forty-eight hours.

To get the girls primed for our mission, I tell them a story I heard about Jack Nicholson and the Bale of Hay Saloon. Nicholson drank in the Bale of Hay while filming scenes for *Missouri Breaks*. At one time he told Ford Bovey it was his favorite saloon.

Ford told me that one night Nicholson was chatting up the attractive young bartender. He was enchanted with her and stayed until closing time, sure he'd score that night. But when she was ready to close, the young woman said her boyfriend was waiting, and she left him cold. Jack wasn't used to that in Hollywood. But, then again, he wasn't in Hollywood. Virginia City is a land unto itself. Ofttimes I have wanted to live there—especially in the winter when the snow encases the town—ghosts and all—in a quiet revelry and the day begins with a trudge through packed white to the single establishment open to serve the locals.

ONE SHORT WINDOW

The Bale of Hay had another bar in the back when I first visited. That back bar is my main memory of the Bale of Hay, and it no doubt was lost in the fire. It was a few steps up from the main room—a haunted nook with a low ceiling, no windows, old oak tables, and heavy captain's chairs—built when the average height of a man was somewhere around five feet. I remember how the place smelled old. With a faint tug at the imagination one could smell the yeast from the bread dough. This room once was part of what Ford Bovey told me was the oldest building in Virginia City. It was a mechanical bakery, mechanical meaning they used a machine to stir the dough. It was this bar Jack Nicholson once called his favorite saloon and it was here they shot scenes with Dustin Hoffman for *Little Big Man*.

When I visited before, I noticed tourists didn't stay long in the Bale of Hay. They'd poke their heads in, maybe take a walk through. Ford confirmed my suspicions. His clientele was more local than tourist. This saloon was a little too real. Its furnishings were rich, elaborate, and stylish for their time. But they were neither pretty nor comfortable in any modern sense. There was barely room to turn around. You had to sit back in one of the heavy oak chairs to really feel the place, and then the feeling hinted of villainy. Henry Plummer and his boys—and the avenging vigilantes. The air was thick, the room musky and dark, lit in high afternoon by one short window.

Bale of Hay Saloon

336 West Wallace, Virginia City

We've just begun to tell all the stories that will unravel over the trip when we pull up in front of the Bale of Hay Saloon. I've got a soft touch for the Bale of Hay from years back. I noted then that in Virginia City's early days one barkeep would provide a fresh bale of hay for patrons' horses at the hitching post in front of his saloon and hence the rather unique name. Not long after my first book came out, the venerable Bale burned down. The fire was caused by a space heater left on to help the floor dry; it was Friday the thirteenth.

This is how it looked to me before the fire:

Still inhabiting the original building in Montana's oldest living town, the Bale of Hay sits behind a fantastic musical arcade of player pianos and other antique mechanized instruments.

A small low door opens into one of the most original saloons one is likely to find anywhere. I'm told the back bar is the oldest in Montana—built in Cincinnati in 1862 and shipped up by riverboat. It seems almost a miniature in comparison to the early-twentieth-century grandeur of new models. Its shining mahogany is intricately carved into knobby spokes and prim circles and worked with three-inch-square mirrors into a pleasing design. The mirrors are peeling, but the wood seems to have been carved yesterday.

In 1986 the saloon was reopened in the same building. The interior had pretty much been decimated, but the hundred-year-old brick building housing it still stood. And they were able to save a player piano and several of the ancient movie-box nickelodeons, which can be viewed in the front, as well as the floor-to-ceiling *Nymphs and Satyrs,* a painting (circa 1888) that was brought to the Bale in 1920 from the Hoffman House Hotel in New York. The original back bar must have perished in the fire.

The painting, antique posters, paraphernalia, and an ancient potbellied stove establish the saloon's historical credentials today, and like my first trip, the Bale has an uneasy quiet—even as people come in and take up stools. It's the eerie feeling I always have at some point when visiting Virginia City. The past has ghosts and they do not sleep peacefully in the Bale of Hay. I remember interviewing Ford Bovey, who inherited Virginia City from his parents, Sue and Charles, and sold it to the state in 1997. I was the only one in the Bale when I talked with him, and the filtered light from a side window could not begin to illuminate either the saloon or the spirits that hung in the air.

Today a few locals come in, and an actor from the Virginia City Players stops in for a cup of tea before the matinee. Ruthie, Courtney, and I order Bloody Marys and walk around to unwind from our hurried trip over. I show them the ancient nickelodeon flickers that I wrote about in my first book:

A nickel and a turn of the arm on oak-boxed moving-picture devices give a customer a look at lewd scenes, strange situations. Men and women together; women together; all sorts of folks together, and brown-toned frames fluttering by as one turns the handle, leaving the viewer slightly short of breath at the end, surprised at the old folks.

The only one working today is titled "Why Men Leave Home." It's not as juicy as the ones I saw earlier. We stroll some more around the large room. The bartender today seems a little annoyed by my questions and that in turn annoys the three of us. It's time to mosey on to the Pioneer, a bar I didn't feature last time, and the only bar open all year in Virginia City.

Pioneer Bar

WALLACE STREET, VIRGINIA CITY

Before we stop in the Pioneer, we walk down the street's wood sidewalks to the Madison County Courthouse, built in 1876, the first courthouse in Montana and the oldest still used for its original purpose. The National Register of Historic Places gives it the designation of "highest significance." Several trials of national interest have played out here in recent years—the triathlete abduction or "Mountain Man" trial, the fight between Charles Kuralt's widow and his mistress over his Montana home, and more recently, a couple's squabble over the fate of the Yellowstone Club, a millionaire's retreat near Yellowstone Park. We walk up the winding staircase and into the nineteenth-century courtroom. In a few short weeks Courtney, a recent grad of Georgetown Law School, will take a job with a Manhattan law firm. She's far from New York today.

Back down the street at the Pioneer, we talk to Bruce, a middle-aged man adept behind the bar, clearly the holder of many secrets. He's been bartending here for fourteen years. He's a little shy about responding to my journalistic questions but admits to having ridden a horse into a bar a time or two. "Why do people do that?" I ask. "I did it because I could," he responds.

Bruce is willing to share one story about the bar, a story I'll hear from two other regulars over the course of two visits to the Pioneer. It goes like this: There was this Washington lobbyist who came to Virginia City and fell in love with the town. He hung out in the Pioneer and got to know "Pegger," a regular. His wife realized one day that it was Pegger's birthday, so she called a florist in D.C. and ordered some flowers. Where should they be sent, the D.C. florist asked. She told him to Pegger at the Pioneer Bar in Virginia City. He wanted more of an address—and name for that matter—but she told him, don't worry, just send them to Pegger at the Pioneer. The man was skeptical, but he called the nearest florist, who was in Bozeman. When he told the florist the request, the response was: "No shit? It's Pegger's birthday? I'll have to send him something." From what I hear, the D.C. florist still hasn't gotten over that one.

The Pioneer could be about any long shot of a bar in Montana. Its mahogany back bar is a classic, with stained glass and a working cooler set in its lower section. Stools line the long bar, with tables and keno machines filling out the space opposite it. Knotty-pine walls hold antique farm implements. Bruce tells me it was the Club Saloon at one time, opened in 1933, after Prohibition was fazed out. But a print of a painting that Ruthie comes up with while talking with a bar regular shows most of Virginia City's locals at the time packed into the bar, which it claims was established in 1867.

In the winter people come in for their morning coffee, Bruce tells us. Soon the Colonel arrives. He has stopped in at the Pioneer two times a day since 1980. The Colonel was a fighter pilot in the Korean War and comes from a line of Montana miners. When he left the service, he returned to Montana and came to Virginia City, where his father owned mines. He's pretty much been here ever since.

A few minutes later I'm talking to the D.C. lobbyist of the Pegger story, who now is a full-time Virginia City resident, Colin Mathews. Colin grew up among the privileged along the Beltway. His father was a press secretary for Bobby Kennedy and also worked for Sargent Shriver. Colin went to a prep school with George W. Bush and later worked on Capitol Hill as an aide to senators and congressman before joining one of those high-priced Washington law firms. He came to Virginia City in 1997 for a three-week visit and that was pretty much it. "I was a Phi Beta Kappa, Stanford," he tells me. "And I learned humility for the first time in my life in the Pioneer Bar."

He bought a house and soon he was living here full time. Now he operates an art gallery, serves on the Montana Heritage Commission, and rides his motorcycle when he's not in the Pioneer—what he calls "the center of the universe." Not long after he came, a group of citizens approached him about running for mayor. He thought it was just one of those things you were supposed to do in a small town—like it was his turn to take the helm. So he did it. What he says he didn't understand was the small-town politics and rancor that can develop when someone comes in, looks at the way things are being done, thinks geez, that's a little backward, or corrupt, or whatever and upsets the apple cart. He'd had enough after four years and didn't run again. "I wanted to be able to bring my wife in here and enjoy life," he tells me. "This is the center of the universe, after all."

I ask him if he's happy in Virginia City. He is. And he thinks he's a good role model for his children. He likes it that "they can see that you don't have to be chained to the treadmill of ambition—that who you are is not what you do or what you make."

I'm hoping the legendary Pegger will show, but he doesn't and it's time we head off. I think Ruthie may have ordered a straight shot when I wasn't looking, Courtney's had a few Bud Lights, and I'm feeling the two draft beers I imbibed. The night is early and we have miles to go before we sleep.

After a trip to Ennis, we'll stop back at the Pioneer on our way to our motel. There I'll run into a gang of

BOB'S PLACE

Bob Gohn was blind and you wouldn't have called his face pretty, but he mixed a good drink and ran his place better than most seeing men managed theirs. When Bob was a young man—like most men living in Virginia City—he tried his luck in the mines. It was a gold and silver mine, the year 1920. Drilling into the rock, he hit a missed hole (a hole loaded with dynamite that was "missed" in the original blast). That's how he "got blasted" as he describes it. Surprisingly enough, he lived through it, but they had to put his face back together and his sight was long gone.

Shortly after the accident Bob got into the bar business. He took over the family store, Content Corner, in 1943, renaming it Bob's Place. Before that it was operated by his grandfather, Robert Vickers. (His other grandfather, George Gohn, was a Virginia City pioneer and a vigilante.)

When we visited in the 1970s, Bob had run the place for more than three decades. The front was a grocery store, the back a bar. A friend, Steve Hinick, and I were ready for a drink: a shot of Jack Daniels, Coke back, and a gin and tonic, please. Right to the spot, Bob pulled out the gin, grabbed a shot glass, held it to his ear, tipped the bottle, and poured gin to the top of the jigger. He heard it fill. Not a drop was spilled. Then he pulled the tonic from a cooler under the bar. Then the bourbon and a Coke from the back cooler. He put the appropriate drinks on the counter in front of us. A buck sixty-five, he said. Steve and I jumped. We'd been mesmerized, watching him. We dug for our wallets only to realize we had no change. Steve told Bob the bill he was handing him was a twenty. Bob's fingers moved up and down the bill, but to our relief he didn't hesitate as he rang up the cash register. He had friends who watched out for him, one of whom was visiting with us at the bar.

Note: Bob's Place is now a sandwich shop.

men from all over the country who worked on the Alaskan pipeline, who get together every few years and do a little traveling. We share some tales about the line; I worked as a laborer on it in the mid-1970s. Then someone is buying us a beer. It's Tim Gordon, a man who lives down the street from me in Missoula. Soon actors and Virginia City Players producer Stacy Gordon come in and it's a party. I had never been in the Pioneer before today and here I am—with all sorts of friends around me. It takes some doing to get out by 10:30, and I have to drive twenty miles to our motel. When we get there (we have a reservation but we haven't checked in), there's a sign saying our room has been left open—just go on in. We do and stretch out on the beds. Mission accomplished.

The Longbranch Saloon
125 EAST MAIN, ENNIS

Who doesn't like Ennis? When I did the first book it was a diamond in the rough—a town set on the edge of the pristine chockfull-of-trout Madison River, with a main street that could have been pulled out of a movie like *High Noon*, worn down by years of weather and dropped in the luscious Ruby Valley. Whirling disease gave the town and area a run for its money in the 1990s, killing off most of the rainbow trout, but the fishery has rebounded and life is good in Ennis again. It's much brighter and cleaner than I remember it. In some ways, it seems like an aging Kitty, that legendary proprietress of the fictional Longbranch— an old lady, with a fresh coat of red lipstick.

We park in front of the Longbranch and walk in. Soon we're talking to the owners, a couple of characters—Wally and Laurie Abrisson. Wally's got a bald head and is wearing a fire-hydrant-yellow T-shirt that says, I KNOW—JUST ONE MORE. He's stout and muscled and close to a foot shorter than his pretty and gregarious wife Laurie. I think when looking at her that she's got the right height to be a bartender, taking easy command of her post as she chides Wally for talking while she does most of the work.

Wally was a heavy equipment operator and lived all over the country and in some other countries before deciding to come back to Montana and buy the Longbranch. He says bars had been a "family undertaking" for years and "it was my turn to own a bar." He says he grew up in Ennis, and the Longbranch was the first place he ever tended bar. Of course, he did his share of drinking there, too. "I've paid for the bar on this side and on that side," he says.

Wally met Laurie in Seattle, where she was in school, one quarter away from becoming a registered nurse. Somehow he talked her into marrying him and joining him behind the plank in this bar. She still shakes her head when thinking about the decision, but it's clear she has no regrets.

She tells me you have to see a bar as a community center—you have to take care of people. And that is new to her, coming from a city. She says she prepares a Thanksgiving dinner for Longbranch regulars and others who want to come. "That's what you do here," she

NO KISS & TELL

A few old-timers were sitting in the Silver Dollar in Ennis one afternoon. One guy was bragging about his encounters with a certain woman. The woman heard of it, came straight to the bar, pulled out a pistol, and shot the guy in the stomach. The man fell out the door of the bar, knelt on the ground holding his stomach, looked at the wound, said by golly she did shoot me, and fell dead on Ennis' main street. The woman went free.

The young men who related the incident to me—the Longbranch's friendly bartender and an Ennis local—said the law was on the woman's side, because in Montana, "you can't kill and tell."

says, shrugging her shoulders. Last year, a young man's car broke down in the snow near Ennis on Thanksgiving. He came into the bar to find turkey, dressing, mashed potatoes, and gravy to enjoy along with his beer. "He was pretty happy," Laurie says.

We tell her we're planning on stopping at the Pony Bar and she tells us how much she likes the owners there. When we leave she gives me a Longbranch drink token and tells me to take it to Paula in the Pony Bar and ask her if it will work there. I tuck it in my pocket and promise to stop in the next time I'm in Ennis, which I hope won't be long.

The next day we stop in at Chick's in Alder and at a historic saloon in Nevada City that's just for looks these days. Walking into Chick's we find a young bartender and a few locals. The bartender cards Ruthie and Courtney, which I find amusing because it's clear she's younger than either of them. But she's fun and does her best to entertain us with stories about the locals, notably an old hunter who will remain unnamed.

Chick's is a classic country establishment, with a large U-shaped bar, plenty of room for dancing, impressive longhorn and elk racks, a perimeter boasting pretty diamond-shaped windows, and no less than three hundred brands neatly burned into glowing knotty-pine walls.

We've just downed a formidable breakfast and my companions are ready for Bloody Marys. I settle for my usual draft ale.

The young bartender is telling stories about the old hunter. It's clear he's also a good storyteller; the regulars are waiting for him to stop by the bar. He has a bar route that starts in Sheridan and ends in Ennis. The old guy claims to be pretty much blind, according to the bartender. The funny thing, she says, is that "when it comes to poaching, he can see." Some regulars nod at her stories, laughing at the old man's "selective vision." He's always showing up in town with moose and elk in the back of his truck. But "he guts them all, cuts them up, and gives the meat away," the bartender says. That makes it okay in Alder, if you take this small group as a sampling of public opinion.

Pony Bar

Uptown, Pony

You can buy all kinds of things at the Pony Bar—pizzas, corn dogs, dog treats, eggs ($2.75 a dozen), Pony Bar hats, Pony Bar thongs. Yes, thongs. The display for them is still around, but the thongs are long gone. "They went like crazy," says bartender Paula. "Are you going to order more?" I ask. She rolls her eyes and says, no way.

One of Ruthie's main reasons for coming on this trip is to visit the Pony Bar. In fact, she's been chatting up the Pony Bar for some time. She stopped here years ago on a camping expedition that went astray. The Pony remained as a fond memory. Coming in, it feels like an old, kind sanctuary, its removal from the world the reason for its persistence.

The Pony is all that is left of a mining town born in the late 1860s that once was home to about 5,000 people, with a town meeting hall (the building now housing the bar), Chinese laundries, schools, banks, and saloons. Its name has its origin in mining, not ranching, culture. In 1866 a small man, less than five feet tall, who had been pushed out of finds in Virginia and Nevada Cities, found the first gold on the far edge of the Tobacco Root Mountains. But he was a wanderer, and after taking enough gold dust and nuggets to get him to his next venture, he left. Miners who flocked to the area when they heard of the diminutive miner's success were to have a difficult time pinning a name to the man. Some said Tecumseh Smith, others Smith Tecumseh, still others said his name was McCumpsey. Generally, the tiny man answered to the name Pony, so Pony it was.

The building housing today's Pony Bar was originally a house of ill repute. Beginning in the early 1900s, when mining went bust, it became Bert's Pony Bar. Bert Welch was known for closing the bar promptly at six in the evening, no matter how many people were there. It went through a few hands after she died.

Scott Lambert bought the bar a few years back and has made it a community center. There's a conviviality and unspoken commonality among the people who take up bar stools in the low-ceiling pine-paneled rooms. Today a couple traveling through in their camper from Washington State arrive and order a pizza, clearly familiar with almost everyone in the bar. They come every summer.

Paula isn't particularly happy when I pull out the wooden drink chip from the Longbranch and ask if it will work, but she gets all three of us a drink, leaving any animosity to Laurie. "Payback's a bitch," she says. It isn't long before we're chatting like old friends. Turns out there's a very female side to the Pony Bar, which is rather novel to all three of us.

Paula is telling us about the many events the Pony hosts: a Memorial Day Duck Race (438 people this year), Pony Days, Customer Appreciation Day, Cabin Fever Days (a swimsuit contest, piña coladas). There's a big Halloween party, meals for Thanksgiving and Christmas, Monday Night Football, and a St. Patrick's Day party. The bar also functions as a VFW post and hosts funeral gatherings, wedding receptions, and baby showers.

While we're talking about all these events, an attractive middle-aged woman comes in. Paula notes the bar is still dressed up for the Fourth of July and says she'll have to change it soon. "How about Back to School?" the woman suggests. She lives down the road from the tiny town of Pony and stops into the bar regularly—probably too often, she says, but she isn't the typical barfly. She talks to Paula about artwork donated for an auction at the upcoming Pony Homecoming celebration. Soon, another woman of similar age comes in. "Whew," she says. "I got the pigs back in." In a town the size of Pony everyone knows when the pigs are out.

"How'd you get 'em back in?" I ask. "Tricked 'em," she says, "with popcorn and apples. They love that." Critters tend to run wild in Pony, a town about six miles off the main road from Harrison in a picture-postcard setting of Tobacco Root Mountains rising abruptly above the main street. One fall people were sitting in the Pony when someone noticed a small herd of cow elk were walking down the street past the bar. Someone called out, "Anyone got a cow elk tag?" Anyone who did was up in the mountains hunting, so the elk paraded through Pony unscathed.

The Pony allows dogs—if they behave themselves, which often is not the case. At one celebration Paula counted twenty-three dogs in the bar, and some were getting in fights. She hollered, "Anything with a tail—out of here!"

Scott tells Paula to give each of us a drink token. I'm driving, so I pocket mine. I talk some with Scott, who managed a few bars before buying the Pony about six years ago. When asked why he wanted to buy the saloon, the answer is someone had to do it. But I don't believe him. I think he loves owning the Pony Bar.

It's getting toward six and I know I have more than three hours of driving left in this two-day venture. More women come in, taking up one end of the bar. They seem to be beckoning us into an evening of fun, but unfortunately, we have to go. Reluctantly, I push myself away from the bar, hold up the drink token to Paula, and say, "Next time I'm in Ennis, I'm taking this to the Longbranch."

8

DEER LODGE, ANACONDA, AND OVANDO

There was a dog named Bugsy and he had a tab at the Corner Bar in Deer Lodge. Bugsy would wait outside until someone came to the bar and opened the door. He'd lope in, jump up on a bar stool, and wait for his jerky. His person had told the owners of the bar to give him what he wanted, so they did. Bugsy, a black mutt with an eye patch, is immortalized in a ceiling tile near the front of the bar. And so he should be.

The Corner Office
402 MAIN STREET, DEER LODGE

Pam Meagher Ingraham, the daughter of the man who owned the Corner Bar for several decades, is tending bar today and is the one who tells us about Bugsy. Kelly and I take the story as a cue and go get our dog Bailey out of the car. He struts in and immediately joins Pam behind the bar, where he is given a piece of jerky. Of course, this makes him want to return to Pam every few minutes. She doesn't mind, but we lure him out and show him the water bowl in the back for visiting canines. He drinks to his heart's content.

Henry Meagher and his wife, Ada, sold the Corner Bar a few years ago to a young couple, the Sheltons, who now call it the Corner Office. Pam is an attractive middle-aged woman who some of the bar patrons compare in looks to Sarah Palin, who has just burst onto the national scene. Pam tends bar on Saturdays. "I grew up in this bar. I took one shift and I realized I missed it—a lot." But she's not interested in the night shift. "There's a whole different clientele at night. I couldn't do it with all these kids."

The Sheltons sold the back bar, a classic, and put in a new bar on the opposite side of the space. It's attractive and open, and Pam says it's much easier to work than the old bar, but it definitely changes the ambience. Pam tells

THE LAST SHEEPHERDER

Years ago when I first visited the Corner Bar, I was lucky enough to talk to one of the last sheepherders in Montana—Fred Lenning—a nearly toothless, good-natured old guy who frequented the Corner Bar when he wasn't out watching sheep. Fred told me about one day when Deer Lodge was celebrating its annual rodeo. Fred was a young boy, standing outside the Corner Bar. His father was a gambling man, tending business inside. A cowboy rode up to young Fred and bet him ten dollars he couldn't ride his horse through the bar. Fred took the guy up on the bet, jumped on the horse, and was making good headway through the bar when his father spotted him.

Fred's dad strode up to the horse, yelling at his son all the way; when he reached them he grabbed the horse's tail and yanked on it in an attempt to stop the two and discipline Fred. When he learned his son was in the process of winning ten bucks, the man dropped the horse's tail and congratulated his boy.

When I spoke with him Fred was retired. His family had owned a large sheep ranch before his father had gambled it away, so it was logical for one of the last sheep ranchers in the Deer Lodge Valley to ask Fred if he was available to watch sheep. At that time his boss was the only man who ran as much as a band of sheep (about one thousand head). A young man would have had trouble living on the $400 Fred earned a month, but with his pension, Fred said he did fine.

Watching sheep was great work for a man his age, Fred told me. "I watch sheep, sit on a rock, eat, watch sheep, read a paper if he brings it, sit on a rock, watch sheep. . . ." Fred was due to begin several weeks with the woolies. He told me a young guy had been watching them, but the guy couldn't stay out too long. He liked to be in town for the weekends to chase the girls. Fred didn't mind missing weekends in town, he said, adding he was too old to chase the women. Then with a sly grin, he put in a word for the sheep: "I like them four-legged blondes."

us that her parents were once offered $65,000 for the back bar. The Sheltons put it on e-Bay and didn't know enough to choose the option that would have allowed them to withdraw their item from the bidding; it sold for $20,000—to the highest bidder—a Texan who put it in his basement. Ah well.

This is what I wrote about the back bar many years ago:

The Corner's back bar is unique in my travels. A square stained-glass motif in green and yellow is inlaid through the long, oak casing of the back bar and accompanying lights. The back bar and matching plank and liquor cabinets are solid oak, made by Brunswick around the turn of the century, first used in the Crystal Bar in Anaconda. The plank is systematically scarred, etched throughout with deep nicks from customers pounding their coins into the wood in an attempt to get the barkeep's attention.

Earlier during this visit, I had asked Pam's dad if he was related to Thomas Francis Meagher, who is immortalized, along with his horse, in a granite statue in front of the state capitol. He had said he was, but really didn't know much about the man. Meagher was a freedom fighter in Ireland. He was tried for sedition by the United Kingdom and banished from the isle. He made his way from Australia to America, where he studied law and journalism and later became a Civil War hero, leading the Irish Brigade. He came to Montana after the war and

again became a leader of men as the state's first territorial governor, only to drown in the Missouri River in 1876 at the age of forty-three. Some say he was intoxicated and fell off a steamboat, so he's often referred to as a sort of eccentric, drinking Irishman when other evidence might suggest he was brave, strong in his convictions, and perhaps a little foolhardy, but far from stupid. I mention the story to Pam. Her reply: "If he was a Meagher he was probably drunk."

I tell Pam that the last time I was there I interviewed a sheepherder. "They're pretty much obsolete these days," she says, adding her father used to rent rooms upstairs to sheepherders, a common practice in many old bars.

The Corner is a good-size bar, with a side room for poker games and keno machines. Drinks are cheap. You can get a draft pint of Kokanne for two bucks. Today the place is slowly filling with regulars in the early afternoon. Everyone knows Pam. Some of them no doubt have come just to chat with her. It's an easy place to settle into, especially when you have a happy dog curled up next to your bar stool. But this is our first stop of the day and a September sun pierces the bar's front window, beckoning us back to the road. Anaconda's legendary watering holes await us.

Club Moderne
801 EAST PARK STREET, ANACONDA
This bar is easy to find. It's been photographed every which way but loose. That's because its classic

art deco front is extremely photogenic, especially at night. One of my favorite photos is a stark black and white by John Smart, taken one night in 1983. It places the bar on the corner of Park and Ash, the neon symmetry of the front framed by a glowing BAR sign running down the side street—the structure rounded, all elements intricately fitted, quietly impressive in its clean geometry. But it also can be stunning in dusk, its rounded Carrara glass and black, ivory, and gray polished slate cradled with pastel slivers of neon light and topped with the glowing sans-serif script of Club Moderne. Kelly and I enter through the door, ornate with stainless-steel circles intersected by vertical lines. I have often wondered why I didn't include the Moderne in the first book. I've thought it probably wasn't open then, but I'm to learn it opened in 1937 and has stayed open.

Its architecture alone makes it worthy of note. Designed by Bozeman architect Fred Willson and built by a twenty-something John "Skinny" Francisco, the Club Moderne is "the ultimate expression of the machine age," according to a Montana Historical Society plaque in the bar. Skinny wanted to introduce a new sort of class to Anaconda once Prohibition was lifted, and the Moderne reflects the sinewy, urban style of the late 1930s. In those days the bartenders wore white shirts, black vests, and neckties, and people dressed to the nines when they came to the club. It was a different atmosphere from most of the other Anaconda bars; today the bar holds its style, but draws all sorts.

We order drinks and settle in, taking in the unerring details of art deco design. The perfect geometry of the back bar, the copper and aluminum checkerboard ceiling, the stainless-steel accents, the angles and lines in inlaid wood, the chromium and leather furniture—all the details—all preserved.

I wander into the back room, much larger than the tidy tucked-in-front Gentleman's Lounge, and find another bar, booths, tables, and, again, the original chrome-and-leather chairs. Now the room is used for community events. Once reserved for the ladies, each booth is still outfitted with the original jukebox and a buzzer to herald a bartender. When the Montana legislature passed a bill outlawing women "entertaining" in bars in 1907, Butte and Anaconda dealt with the problem by providing side or back rooms for the women. This is by far the most impressive of the many ladies' lounges I've seen.

Coming back, I note there are two restrooms marked GENTLEMEN in stainless-steel lettering on different walls off the main bar. I'm beginning to need a loo myself, so I'm wondering why the guys rate two and I can't seem to find one. Then I realize the Women's is in the back room.

Tucked away in the back corner of the large expanse is a hot-pink dressing room with an enclosed toilet stall and a sweet little vanity. Nothing seems to have been altered since 1937. A cylindrical stainless-steel light with opaque glass casts a rosy glow over the now frumpy, once chic decor. A trip to the Moderne is worth it if only for a trip to the Ladies. I can't speak for the Gentlemen's. Kelly said they were okay. But then, he's a man and they often don't pay a lot of attention to loos.

Back at the bar, I talk a little with the bartender. She's been in an animated conversation with some friends who have come in, but she's also keeping an eye on us. I ask her about the owners, and she tells me they're John and Stephanie Heckel. They bought the Moderne in 1997 from Skinny's nephew and did some cleaning up and restoration, and in 1999 they had a second grand opening.

The Owl

819 East Third Street, Anaconda

It's fun to walk down Third Street in Anaconda, where streetcars once carried men from the smelter. Every other block there'd be a streetcar stop—and a bar. Thirty years ago I told of the shift change at four in the afternoon, when the men working at the smelter boarded buses that ran the same route as the streetcars:

> *When the men walk in the door of the Owl, a bottle and a beer chaser are there to greet them. Dick puts the bottle on the bar and the men pour their own shots. Three shots and a beer chaser go for $1.55. This low price is in line with prices in many of the old bars in Butte-Anaconda, where any bar worth its salt buys every third drink.*

It's still pretty much that way today—a bar every other block—but the smelter has been closed down

A MORNIN'S MORNIN

Nowhere else in the state is the after-work drink revered as it is in Butte-Anaconda. There is a deep-seated belief in both towns that whiskey drunk after a shift of breathing rock dust underground or fighting the fumes of the smelter is as medicinal as a daily vitamin. That first well-earned shot purges the throat, brings a cleansing tear to the eye, and fights its way down through the weary, embattled throat and lungs down to the abdomen, where it settles in a warm, healing pool and from there sends out a message to the brain that all is much righter with the world than it was an hour before. Another shift has been pulled.

for years and drinks are slightly more expensive. Today the Owl is packed with people at three on a Saturday afternoon, and it's a rowdy crowd. I had been impressed before because the Owl, which has been in operation since the late 1890s, had no bar stools:

Old photos of Montana saloons show men bellied up to the bar, boot on the rail, no bar stool in sight. I'm not sure when the stool was introduced, but I have a theory. With Prohibition, many of the bars took to selling ice cream, Hire's root beer, and other such frivolous refreshments. The old photos confirm Montana pioneers believed alcohol was made for drinking standing up, but it must have seemed silly to stand, foot on the rail, to sip a soda or dig into a mound of ice cream. The bar stool came in with ice cream and soda pop, I will contend, and the furniture remained after Prohibition ended. Today it is difficult to find a saloon without the stools. But the past dies slowly in Anaconda. There I found a bar where stools have neither seen the light of fluorescent bulbs nor felt the spray of a draft: the Owl on Third Street.

I must report that bar stools have made it into the Owl. And the bar has changed in ways that aren't particularly positive for me, but the regulars seem more than happy with it. I see the straight-back wood booths in the large side room, once the ladies' lounge—there from time immemorial it would seem, although the wall between the lounge and the main bar has been removed. A shuffleboard that came to Montana on a steamboat, making

it more than a hundred years old when I first visited, is being used as a kind of storage area. A photo of FDR still hangs above the bar. A beautiful Regulator grandfather clock lends grace to the raucous atmosphere. I'm glad the Owl is still open, but curious to see what's happened to Sladich's, so it's time to push on.

Sladich's
600 EAST THIRD STREET, ANACONDA

Mautz Sladich was a favorite of mine when I did the first book. He would be in his nineties today, so I'm not expecting to find him. I'm not even sure his bar will be open, but we see the sign and make a quick right to park on the side street where a 1930ish mural of stylish people drinking cocktails and smoking cigarettes still graces one outside wall.

Inside we find two men at the end of the bar and a woman behind the plank. We see a boisterous lab on a leash, and I ask if I can bring our dog in. They say sure. Bailey is having a very good day.

Everything in Sladich's has changed. Mautz had remodeled the bar when I visited him, but it was full of memorabilia and his special touch. Much of it is gone today. Jill Morley tells me Mautz died in 1997, and his nieces and nephews tried to keep the bar open but decided to sell it a few years ago. An accounting student at Montana Tech in Butte, Jill was looking to buy an affordable house in Anaconda. She called about buying or renting the apartment upstairs and was asked if

HAPPY DAYS

The first thing I saw in Mautz Sladich's place thirty years ago was a full-color portrait of FDR sitting over the cash register. I told Mautz that it seems FDR is found in every bar in Butte and Anaconda. "Sure," said Mautz, "that's because he gave the country back to booze." Three men drinking at the bar formed a chorus in agreement, rather surprised I could be so dense. I had thought it might be because of the New Deal.

How silly of me.

Mautz closed at six back in those days. It was his bar and he wasn't getting any younger. He felt like closing at six to go upstairs and have dinner with his wife, Rose, and so he did. But when he was open, it would have been difficult to find a bartender more gracious than this laughing Croatian. With nearly every shot he poured for one of his friends, Mautz poured one for himself. During the hour I spent with him, I saw him tip many shots; yet any effect the liquor had on him was not apparent. He was one of the healthiest-looking sixty-year-old men I'd ever seen. With every shot came a toast. His customers may forget, but Mautz never did. Ritual, grace, style, brotherhood; with every tip of the glass, Mautz saluted life. The toasts varied that day, but the most common was "Happy Days."

she'd like to buy the whole building, including the bar. She went for it.

"What about accounting?" I ask. "Oh, I'll probably do that at some point," she says. "I'm not a sitter."

She claims the bar is haunted, and I wouldn't be surprised if Mautz is hanging around. "Every time we make a change, stuff falls off the walls," Jill says. She says one day she was doing something behind the bar and a stereo speaker jumped from a secure shelf on the wall and landed several feet away—on the bar plank. There had been nothing to cause the movement. She says she straightens photos hanging on the wall only to come down the next morning to find them noticeably ajar. The next morning they'll be hanging straight again.

Jill tells me that the family took most of Mautz's mementos, which he had enjoyed showing me on my first visit:

The Sladiches have owned the building and the bar since before the turn of the century, and Mautz has old-time photos and paraphernalia to prove it. Most of it is in what he calls the garbage case. Some of the antiques and collectibles were brought in by Sladich's patrons, but much of it was gathered by the family. There's a KEEP COOL WITH COOLIDGE sign in the case; photos of the bar's grand opening in 1896; an old harmonica; an English leather cribbage board; a button hook; a raffle ticket from 1897; and an eighteen-inch Nazi dagger in a scabbard and a Nazi Cross, both of which Mautz claims

he took off dead Nazis, along with some authentic Hitler stamps. There's also an American flag folded in the classic style. I ask him about it. It was the flag draped over the casket of a close friend. The man was a bachelor who spent a good deal of time with Mautz in the bar. Sladich's was probably as close to home as any place for the man, and Mautz was his best friend. When the man died Mautz took care of the funeral arrangements and, since there was no widow to claim it, he was given the flag.

Today I think of how much Mautz enjoyed his stuff. We have a few draft beers and chat with Jill and her husband, Tuffy, and his friend Eddie from Oklahoma. Jill tells me Mautz had been in medical school and wanted badly to be a doctor but was called home after a death in the family to run the bar. That explains what I saw years ago—a gracious melancholy, a sense of what could have been.

A few single men come and go while we're there, but I'm getting the feeling that Jill and Tuffy are like Mautz. They mainly keep the bar open in order to chat with their friends. "We open at two and close when we want to," Jill says. "And we're closed Sundays and Mondays."

Another thing that is familiar is the cost of the drinks. Butte and Anaconda always have had the lowest-priced drinks around, and today I'm feeling an old comfort level. The draft pint I'm drinking is two dollars; I could get a tap Rainier pint for a buck, twelve ounces for fifty cents. Those are almost like 1970s prices.

I notice the back room and don't really remember it from my first visit. I ask Jill if it had been the ladies' lounge. "We had eighty-year-old women coming in and sitting in the booths back there when I first bought the bar," Jill says. She goes on to say they took all but one of the booths out and put a pool table in the room. "We needed to modernize," Jill says. What a shame, I think. Eighty-year-old women still interested in meeting at Sladich's place and they're run out.

Tuffy takes me out back and shows me the boardinghouse that the Sladiches owned and ran for years—and some outhouses that had toilet seats and levers for "flushing," but no water—an interesting transition to indoor plumbing, which was not available to those living in the boardinghouse at the time.

A couple of young girls come in and head straight for the bar. One asks what a Coke costs. Jill says a dollar. The girl says, will you take sixty cents? Jill says yes and sells her a Coke. I laugh when they leave, noting how Anaconda kids learn early how to barter. "We usually give them Cokes and chips after school," Jill says. "If you're nice, they won't pelt your windows."

Trixi's Antler Saloon

HIGHWAY 200, OVANDO

I'm sitting in Trixi's thinking of legends. Trixi McCormick certainly was one, a nationally known trick roper and horseback rider who retired to her home state and opened this bar decades ago. She could play harmonica and tap dance and spin two ropes—all at the same time. She entertained in rodeos, vaudeville, movies, nightclubs, and theaters and joined Bob Hope on USO tours. At the age of eighty, she could still spin an eighty-foot rope. Her given name was Ethel Stokes.

Then there was Jim Crumley, a mystery writer, who became known in western Montana and beyond for his trenchant plots and irascible private eyes and their wild ways—as well as for his own prodigious bar time. Crumley died a few weeks before my visit to Trixi's and I've been thinking about him.

Today the bartender notes that there was this guy in here with a French woman a year or two ago. I know immediately the guy was Crumley and how it happened. Jim's wife Martha had told me recently about a film a French company had made of Crumley in his favorite bars. The French loved Crumley and his books. And they loved Montana author Jim Welch and his books—so much that they knighted him. Crumley was not exactly the kind of guy likely to be knighted by the French, but he was the kind of guy able to attract a film crew to join him in visiting his favorite watering holes.

I've driven up from Missoula with my two ski buddies, Dianne and Peg. Pulling into the parking lot we end a three-minute discussion of men, encapsulating the male psyche in a paragraph. A decade or two before this, we would have spent most of the trip up deciphering the animal.

It puts us in the mood for a drink. We belly up to the bar and order lunch and refreshments. I look around and don't notice anything that different from years before. I've stopped in Trixi's many times in the last few decades. It's a comfortable niche in a changing world, a magnate to travelers along the Blackfoot River Valley. Two guys sit by a window to my side, drinking coffee and reading a newspaper. A father and young son stop in for an orange soda on the way to the little guy's soccer game.

A trip to the side room shows they've renovated a little there, where they can seat a group of twenty or so for their legendary steak dinners. A traveler pays his bill and heads out. Soon the doors are flung open and the quiet is broken by a string of people massing in. A couple women join us at the bar and are buying Trixi T-shirts and sweatshirts. There's quite a commotion with what looks like fifteen to twenty people suddenly in the place.

I ask the women where they're from. We learn they're out from Washington, D.C., for the U.S. Fish, Wildlife and Parks. They've been touring the area. Peg and Dianne challenge a couple of the men in the group to foosball. Peg, an excellent telemark skier, also happens to be a whiz at foosball. When the women win handily I'm proud. One of the guys asks Peg, "Have you done this before?" Some people can be kind of dense when out of their element, I think. Of course, Trixi probably would have won if she had been around, too. She no doubt had the wrists and reflexes for it.

I talk some with the bartender, Loretta, who has worked at Trixi's for close to eight years. She talks about how the saloon acts as a restaurant for the area and how important that is for people. There's not another place to eat in at least a twenty-mile radius—just like it was thirty years ago. They serve breakfast, lunch, and dinner. Sunday is a big day, she notes. "Church people always like to go out for breakfast."

I had interviewed Trixi a year after she sold the bar in the late 1970s. It wasn't an easy telephone interview; I suspect it would have been a totally different story had I caught her in the bar. She was known for her hospitality, straightforward style, and her cooking. Then she told me she had been drawn to trick roping when she was fifteen years old. Bob Rooker, a famous trick roper, told her there weren't many women who could trick rope, and it might be a good gig for her.

Trixi needed no more encouragement. She began to work with the rope. She practiced her way into fairs and rodeos, then to a vaudeville act, a USO show in Mexico City, to the Royal Rodeo Show in Sydney, Australia, the Cow Palace in San Francisco, then television. "You Asked for It" asked for Trixi. Then she did stunts in movies. Trixi not only threw a mean rope, she did it off the back of a horse.

I had asked her about the bullet hole in the ceiling. "Ah, he was just playing," Trixi explained. (She kept a single-action Colt behind the bar and was known to use it occasionally when customers or boyfriends didn't toe the line.)

Trixi's in Ovando remains a comfortable niche in a changing world.

When the crowd finally leaves, I mosey around the room to see how much is left from thirty years ago. I had written about the antiques and oddities Trixi had collected, many of them from people living in the area. The pump organ is still there and the same mounted heads and a few gilded frames. I see a newspaper article that appeared in the *Missoulian* after Trixi's death in 2001. It notes how she would take Silver Dollar, her last horse, everywhere with her—including into elevators and, of course, into the bar. He'd eat popcorn and drink beer, tipping the can to get at it.

Trixi had moved to California to live with her son prior to her death. He reported that she remained in good physical shape almost until her death, but she had Alzheimer's. She kept trying to get back to Montana, he said. She'd say, "I've got to get dressed. I've got a show to do." The Associated Press reported she was ninety-one when she died. Her granddaughters, who threw the wake for her in Drummond, said Trixi had made it clear that her age was never to be discussed. They were concerned when her age got out. "She'll haunt us," one said.

I think again of legends. Trixi retired after twenty years of trick roping and returned to Montana, where she created a haven for herself, her family, and others; she inherently understood the life span of an athletic career. Crumley was a writer until the end. I remember seeing him in his favorite spot one night at the Depot in Missoula.

He was going to Los Angeles for an awards ceremony. He had been included with all the kitchen-table names of mystery writers for some award and was excited, in the contained but almost little-boy way Crumley would get excited. He said he didn't expect to win, but it would be fun to go. I told him that I liked his work better than any of the others and that he should win. He just brushed that aside, thinking I was full of it. But I meant it. His mysteries were finely wrought, touched with the heart and soul of real people, often taking the reader to the edge and dangling her over it but always in the most interesting way, with a subtlety not often found in mysteries. Toward the end of his life, people were recognizing his considerable contributions to the mystery genre.

Sometimes I'd catch myself watching Crumley watching people in the Depot or Charlie's. He was always gathering material. He had no qualms about the difficulty of his task. One time he told me that every time he finished a book he would realize he'd have to come up with another idea and spend a few more years on a book, and he'd think of other possible professions he could have pursued—perhaps being a veterinarian. Which, of course, we both knew was preposterous. Jim was a writer because he was good at it, it was what he did, his life—and because he needed the money.

When we leave, I see the sign is still there. Hanging from the archway, a worn three-by-four-foot piece of wood, its white paint fading: THANK YOU, FRIEND.

9

ALONG THE YELLOWSTONE RIVER

I enjoyed my first October bar trip so much that I slated October for my long sojourn into southeastern Montana. The weather looks to be fairly good and who knows what it will be later in the month, so I've loaded up my laptop, iPod, cell phone, camera, purple satchel, notebooks, dog food, and treats—and my dog Bailey—and we're off.

Bailey is my only friend willing to take a week to explore the Yellowstone Valley and beyond with me. Truth is, he has no choice. But he will turn out to be an agreeable traveling companion. He is especially good at giving yearning looks out the side window when I pull into motels looking for a place to stay. God knows, he needs out of that backseat after logging close to three hundred miles a day and waiting for me as I spend countless hours on bar stools. He's a good dog, yes he is.

Waterhole Saloon
209 DIVISION STREET, REED POINT

We've come nearly three hundred miles from Missoula when we turn off Interstate 90 and drive into Reed Point. Various renovations of buildings are under way and it's clear the town is trying to save its past. Years ago Chris Hahn had told me Reed Point was once the biggest town on the Yellowstone River—before Billings or Livingston were established.

A 1916 Reed Point newspaper listed several banks, lumberyards, and five or six saloons, Chris had told me then. "We had our own dentists, doctors, and attorneys. It was quite the place."

I take Bailey for a brisk walk about the town in the warmth of a setting sun and check out various renovation projects, then open the door of the Waterhole Saloon to find a middle-aged woman cooking something that's beginning to smell pretty good in the small kitchen in the back. After securing a beer, I tell her why I'm visiting. She remembers the first book immediately, and it brings back memories of Otis, the bar pig I wrote about then. I ask if she's Chris's wife and the answer is yes—Diana Hahn, an attractive woman, Gros Ventre Indian, and chief proprietor of the Waterhole today. She says she "retired Chris," although he still provides wood for the stove and fixes equipment when it's down.

This is the third saloon I've found in my search to have the same proprietors as in my first visit, and that always cheers me. The place is much the same, but like Diana and me, decades older. Chris built the bar in the early 1970s, modeling it on the Jersey Lilly in Ingomar—down to the wood-plank sidewalk in front. I wrote then: "Inside is a haven of wood—ponderosa pine, juniper, redwood, oak—all kinds of wood, worked into bar stools, chairs, tables, walls, the plank, and back bar. And the smell is wood, from the old schoolhouse stove that heats the large room."

The mosaic of wood still forms the interior of the Waterhole today, although it's not as shiny and new as in my first visit. What hasn't changed is the warmth and fragrance of burning wood in the old stove. Of course, the first topic of discussion is Otis. "He'd (Otis) get drunk and go to sleep behind the stove," Diana tells me. "He was an alcoholic." She says people still try to bring all kinds of critters into the bar. "We've had sheep in here. We've had goats, horses—just about everything," she says. A sign above the bar draws the line: NO SERVICE WILL BE PROVIDED AT THIS BAR TO ANYONE ON A HORSE.

Diana has paid tribute to her people with photos and tribal paraphernalia around the bar. I see she is selling braided sweetgrass for three dollars a braid. One sign informs: INDIANS DISCOVERED COLUMBUS. Another informs ALL NATIONS WELCOME—EXCEPT CARRIE, in a reference to the militant leader of the temperance movement, a woman known for taking hatchets to bars and the people in them. "She was a nut," Diana says.

My eyes keep returning to an oil painting center stage behind the bar. It's a reclining nude—an alluring and mysterious woman who could have been Diana at the age of eighteen or nineteen. I wonder if Diana posed for it when she was young. I think about asking her, but decide not to. It doesn't really matter if it's her or not. It's a nice variation on the turn-of-the-century pink-cheeked veiled lady.

Diana tells me about the sheep drive she and Chris helped establish in Reed Point as a response to the statewide 1989 cattle drive celebrating Montana's Centennial. The sheep drive upstaged the cattle drive, drawing thousands to Reed Point's six-block wood-sidewalk main street in 1989. Some years the drive, which quickly became a full-fledged civic celebration, drew fifteen thousand people on a Labor Day weekend. "Now it's settled down to four thousand," she tells me. It's a major fund-raiser for Reed Point, garnering tourists from miles around who come to see hundreds of sturdy woolies charging down the street in an event some say is akin to the Running of the Bulls in Pamplona, Spain. Wow. I make a mental note to drive over some year for the event. I have no illusions of it being

OTIS THE PIG

"We've had just about every kind of animal in here," said Waterhole owner Chris Hahn when I visited years ago—"goats, ducks, sheep, horses, owls. A couple of weeks ago I had to kill a bat that was dive-bombing the bar."

Until a few weeks before my visit, Otis, the pig, had been the star of the show. Chris bought Otis from a guy passing through Reed Point. He paid two shots of whiskey and a Waterhole bumper sticker. Otis was cute then, only two weeks old. "He was raised in the bar," Chris told me. "He ate peanuts and drank beer. He was drunk all the time. He'd shell the peanuts out and eat 'em."

The next question, obviously, was where is Otis now? "He's been eaten," Chris said. "Wasn't worth a damn to eat. Really bad. We took seventy-five pounds of lard out of him—all that beer and peanuts."

But if he wasn't much of a ham dead, Otis was entertaining while alive. Otis would play with the dogs in Reed Point. "He'd run up and down Main Street," Chris said. "He'd chase the dogs; then they'd chase him." Chris showed me pictures of Otis at the bar and added, "they're a better pet than a dog."

I wondered—since Otis was such a good pet—why they didn't keep him around a while longer and got my answer after asking if Otis still lived in the bar after he was fully grown. "When they're four hundred pounds," Chris said, "it's hard to keep 'em out."

Pamplona but it still must be a sight. Enough to put you in the mood to celebrate one thing or another.

Then there's the Yellowstone Boat Float that takes place on the weekend after the Fourth of July. It's been going on since the late 1960s, and Reed Point is an overnight stop in the Livingston to Columbus float. Diana's not too impressed with this event—"a bunch of drunks and groupies," she tells me. She goes back to check on the Texas-style ribs she's cooking, which are smelling better by the minute. She offers a dinner special every Thursday night. Tonight you can get the ribs, red potatoes, and salad for $12.95.

Like many a great small-town bar, the Waterhole is the only establishment in town that serves food, and Diana is clearly a good cook. She's got a varied lunch and dinner menu. She even serves breakfast on Sunday mornings. She asks if I'd like another beer. I clearly would, but I've got two more stops to make this day and Bailey doesn't drive. A couple of locals come in. One older gentleman orders a Canadian Mist with Mountain Dew. A strange brew, but to each his own. It costs $2.75.

I buy a braid of sweetgrass and tell Diana I'll try to stop in for lunch on my way back to Missoula.

New Atlas Saloon

528 PIKE AVENUE, COLUMBUS

The New Atlas has always been a little special to me. Perhaps because it is so much what it is—without making a big deal of it. A classic saloon, established in 1906, its mahogany parallel back bars are unique in my travels. And, although I could live without taxidermy in bars, there are few authentic old-time saloons without the mounts and stuffed wildlife; the New Atlas stands head and tail over most of the others and could almost achieve museum status with its collection.

I've been here a few times since my first book came out, but there's always a bit of trepidation when I enter. The mantra is I hope they haven't changed it. I hope they haven't changed it.

They haven't. The only thing that's new is the front side room—probably where women drank before they were allowed in the "main house." It's been given over to poker machines.

A sign on entering says, WELCOME, STRANGER. Yes, indeedy. Architecturally, the New Atlas is in the same league as the Montana Bar in Miles City. It's a pleasure just to wander around and take in the mahogany entranceway, the stained glass, the back bars, the sixty-some mounts of all sorts of critters, the pressed-tin ceiling, the past clinging stoically to the walls awaiting the inevitable force of change. If you can make it to the New Atlas before change does, tip one to me, please.

I do a little inventory from what I observed for the first book: the piano is still here, as are the dark wood booths; gone are the spittoons in the bar's footrest and the paperback collection. Before, an old television acted as a bookend to tattered paperbacks. Today there's a few flat-screen TVs, but no one is paying the least bit of attention to them.

Here's how I saw it years ago when the bar was so full on a weekday afternoon I had to stand to have a drink. Much of this holds true today:

Hulking throughout the room are bald eagles, an albino mule deer fawn, a coyote howling to the moon, young bobcats fighting, an Audak (African mountain sheep), a Canadian lynx, a raccoon or two, a fox, a snow owl, moose heads, elk heads—buffalo, antelope, mountain sheep—all kinds of heads—a two-headed calf—and other aberrations of the animal world.

The back bar, a beautiful mahogany reminiscent of the former Turf in Missoula and Great Falls' Club Cigar, dates from 1906. Another back bar—mirrored like the main bar—is positioned opposite the mahogany plank. Sitting at the main bar you can see yourself coming and going in the mirrors of the two bars. You also see dual reflections of all the animals, mounted heads, antlers, etc., and after a few drinks they seem to be coming and going, too.

There is a queer sensation that goes with drinking surrounded by dead, stuffed animals. The first reaction is one of nonchalance—ah, some nice stuffed animals. After a few drinks you feel countless pairs of eyes bearing down. You have another beer to relax under the scrutiny, look around again, and you're among friends, the animals' glares having softened to amused acceptance.

CONVERSATION

The first time I walked into the Atlas thirty years ago it was a little crowded, a little rowdy, but friendly, too, even polite.

A mug of draft beer was as cheap as in Butte, thirty-five cents. "When I Get Over You" was on the jukebox. The clientele was the mix found often in good old-time bars, and much of the conversation was between people who had known one another for so long they hardly looked at one another when they spoke. Their words were spaced with long, thoughtful silences—the conversation of people who have lived, worked, and drunk together for decades in a town no more than a square mile in size . . . Kenny came back with my change. Silver dollars. Real money. I knew I had crossed the Rockies then. Time to push on—through the sun and dust and roll of the Yellowstone River Valley.

I'm enjoying the mirrors again when Leonard, a cabinetmaker who has lived in Columbus for decades, comes in for his nightly after-work cocktail. He sits and we talk a little about the saloon. He was a bartender here a few years back. I ask him how the Atlas came to have so much taxidermy. He tells me the original owner started it, but many of the mounts have been donated by people—some from remote corners of the world.

I note how the back room is a little empty. There was a poker game going that first afternoon I was in, I tell him. "No, I remember those guys," he says. "They were playing Panguigue." Okay.

Leonard says there's still poker but now the games are held in an enclosed back room. The area between the bar and the poker room is turned into a bullpen—that's right, an actual bullpen—and prize yearling bulls are brought in for review during Bo-Bo Days. "They haven't done it in a couple of years," Leonard says. Horses, pigs, sheep—I thought I'd heard of or seen it all. But yearling bulls. That's a new one. Surprise is always good. Especially in an old saloon you might expect to expire gracefully. Here's to Bo-Bo Days.

The Bull & Bear Saloon
19 North Broadway, Red Lodge

I'm having car trouble the next day, so plans to check out several Red Lodge bars will have to be put on hold until I figure out if that damned check engine light is for real or a ruse. I do make it into the Bull & Bear Saloon,

a fine all-purpose old bar with an attached restaurant and a huge dance hall upstairs. The Bull & Bear is a place where the alpine set meets the rancher set. The back bar is reminiscent of Swiss alpine architecture, while around the bar pastel and watercolor art features portraits of local ranchers, cowboys, and cowgirls. A jackalope behind the bar is wearing sunglasses.

Nancy Johnson, the current owner, takes me up the stairs to view the large dance hall. The original bar spans the back wall, with a large stage on the opposite end of the expanse, about the size of a basketball court—quite a place for musical events in a town the size of Red Lodge. It's probably been around a hundred years or more. Nancy tells me about several other bars to check out in Red Lodge—all within a few blocks on the main street—the Red Lodge Cafe, the Snag, and the Snow Creek. I bemoan my luck as I drive past them and out of town. It's Friday and I need to get to Billings, where I can have diagnostics done on the car before venturing farther into the wilds of eastern Montana. It's clear I'll have to come back. Red Lodge, per capita, seems to offer barhopping potential akin to Missoula.

The Jersey Lilly
1 Main Street, Ingomar

The next day, the engine light having been shown to be a rank fake, I'm off early for Ingomar. It's a glorious day. A golden expanse of land married to a blue sky brings up a deep-seated familiarity that feels awfully good. Driving north of Billings to meet up with the Musselshell River, I'm in land like I grew up in. It's not flat and it's certainly not ugly, as some navel-gazing western Montanans may say. It has endless vistas that feature eerily elegant sandstone formations, undulating hills, tree-lined creek beds, rain-sculpted gullies. There's something new coming around every bend. Surprise is the best word for this land. On some days the word might be delight. For me, today, it's like breathing from the bottom of the stomach.

When we pull into Ingomar around noon, the place is hopping. There's a bunch of campers and RVs parked next to the saloon and all kinds of cars and rigs around. I note a new addition to town: Central Park, as declared in an eight-foot black metal archway to a block-size area of packed dirt—Ingomar's idea of communal recreation. There are a couple of tents pitched, a water spigot, a crude rain shelter, and a picnic table. I let Bailey out for a walk, catch up with family on my cell phone, and check to see if the Lilly's hitching post and outhouses are still intact (they are). I find a shady spot under a bench in the park and leave Bailey water and the potential for a nice nap, in sun or shade, his choice.

Then I take a good look at the building. Years before, I wrote this and it's pretty much the same today:

The wood-planked porch and hitching posts haven't changed much in the decades they've been around. The Jersey Lilly rises from them—a sturdy yellow brick (once the town bank), and stands weather-beaten, dust-ridden, age-worn, but unrelenting—a stalwart to the weather-beaten, dust-ridden sheep and cattle men and women she still serves.

Inside the Lilly, I pull up a bar stool and order a beer and a bowl of beans. Ahhh. They're almost as good as when Bill was alive. Bill Sewart, who died a few years before, always had a pot of beans on at the Jersey Lil, and they've kept to the tradition. The bar is full of hunters today, and the pot of beans in a slow cooker rests in an attractive salad bar—definitely something new for the Jersey Lil. I enjoy the food and release from the car for a time and just soak in the atmosphere.

The Jersey Lil hasn't changed much but it does feel different without Bill and that pugnacious face, with a cord around the nose bridge of his glasses, securing them to his head. (He took enough punches in boxing matches in the Navy that he had to hold his glasses on that way.)

It isn't long before I'm talking to another veteran—in this case a veteran of the horse corral, Morris, who works for the man who bought the Jersey Lil from Sewart and saved Ingomar, Jerry Brown.

Brown owns a concrete company in Minneapolis, Morris says, and took a liking to Ingomar. He owns a house on the edge of town and comes out fairly regularly and often sends people from his company to Ingomar for a little dose of western reality. A group of them come in from a horseback ride as I talk with Morris.

Morris takes care of Brown's stable of fourteen horses and a small herd of bison. He also gives stagecoach rides to people showing up in Ingomar, mostly in the summer. His grandparents homesteaded in the Missouri Breaks, and his parents had a ranch out of Jordan. Morris is open, friendly, informed, humorous, and full of the prairie, where he's spent his life. If you want to meet a cowboy, you could do no better than to meet Morris.

I ask him about horseback riding around Ingomar, specifically which direction people usually ride in. "Oh, you can go about any way," is the reply. There is a sense in Ingomar that you're in a place existing before fences—and time, for that matter—dirt, grass, and sky as far as the eye can see. And there's an unhinged freedom to the feeling—expanse, possibility, the unknown. The Jersey Lil is the haven; outside you're on your own. If you're a fan of Larry McMurtry's *Lonesome Dove*, Ingomar is the closest you're likely to get to experiencing that reality today.

Somehow Morris and I get to talking about rodeo-ing. Morris did a little of it in his younger days—team roping and saddle bronc riding—for the prize money. He never rode bulls, however. "No one ever accused me of getting on a bull," he says, adding it's said that bull riders have a size 5 hat and a size 19 shirt. He tells me that after a while, he "figured out the best way to get paid at a rodeo was to go to work." So he rode horses to pick up cowboys who got thrown from bucking horses. He still attends the Miles City Bucking Horse Sale, saying his employer understands that he needs those days off every year—not just the three of the sale, but four or five to allow for socializing and recovery.

He still breaks and trains horses and it's clear he's fond of them. "Nowadays, if a horse has a problem, it's man-made," he tells me. "There's just too many good ones."

He tells me a little about the back bar, one of the prettiest I've seen. He says it came up the Yellowstone on the steamship to Forsyth, unlike many of the other antique back bars in the state, which were brought on the Missouri to Fort Benton. This back bar was stored for years before Bill Sewart's dad bought it for the Jersey Lil. It's as pretty as I remember—one of the prettiest and oldest I've seen: small, ornate cherrywood. The mirrors, beginning to oxidize, are all that hint of its age. The ceiling is a fine old pressed tin painted a rich cream white. The floor is worn wood planks.

Sewart had told me there would never be a television set in the Jersey Lil as long as he was tending bar. There is a television in the bar today. Bill would probably be glad to know it's tuned to a music station.

A man comes in to check about pumping gas from a circa 1960s gas pump across the road from the bar. Colleen, the postmistress for Ingomar and Melstone, is cooking and tending bar today. She fills in at the Lil when they're busy, just to help out. Hunting season is a busy time, so she's here today. She tells the man, just double what it says on the pump (for payment).

☞ **The open sky of eastern Montana offsets the Jersey Lilly in Ingomar.**

INGOMAR

Ingomar, at one time, was the largest sheep-shearing town in the world, according to Bill Sewart, former proprietor of the Jersey Lilly. In the very early days—before fences divided the land—they'd trail sheep east from a good part of central Montana and shear them in Ingomar. Then they'd push the woolies on to Glendive, where they were sent East to a market of immigrants who still preferred mutton to beef.

But Sewart said the homesteaders eventually crowded the big sheep men out. And so Ingomar, once a wool man's boomtown, now seemed deserted until I reached the end of a dusty road—Main Street Ingomar—and saw the proud sign of the Jersey Lilly.

Bill used to serve four cuts of steak, sandwiches, his famous beans cooked in a mildly hot, thin broth, and delicately sliced orange and onion that he insisted you pile on a saltine cracker and eat in one bite. (The combination was surprisingly good.) He sold a wide range of staples, postcards, and general merchandise and pumped gas on the side. He opened at seven in the morning and closed when no one had come in for a spell.

About thirty people lived in Ingomar back then. Shortly after the start of World War II, there were no bars open in the town. They'd closed when so many of the area's young men had gone to war. Bill's father sent his daughter up to the town store to get a pack of cigarettes one evening. She came back empty-handed, saying the store had closed. Bill's dad said, "By golly, when you can't get a pack of cigarettes or a drink in a town at nine o'clock, you'd better do something about it." So he opened the Jersey Lilly in the old bank building, naming it for the famed combination bar/courtroom of Texas hanging judge Roy Bean.

Morris tells me Ingomar now has a bed-and-breakfast. The old schoolhouse has been fit up with rooms and beds to rent. "That's the bed," Morris says. "This is the breakfast." I remember before how Bill complained when they had to put toilets in the school. Today there are modern restrooms for the RV campground next to the Jersey Lil, but the bar still goes with the outhouses.

There's a bit of taxidermy in the Jersey Lil, including a moose-head mount with a cigarette dangling from its lips. I notice a massive bison head that seems to be new. I ask Morris about it. "Yeah," he says, "that guy took a dislike to people." I ask if it was recent. "Oh yeah, last year, I think," Morris says. "He was big," I say. "He was fixing to get bigger" is the response.

A man comes in who drives truck regularly between Portland and Milwaukee. He's plopped a trailer down in Ingomar and stays a day or two on the way out and back. He gets a hearty greeting when he comes in the door and orders up dinner—another soul who has found Ingomar, one of the best-kept secrets in the West. I'm sorry when I have to leave, but I'm a happier person for having been here. As I drive south I imagine a reunion of friends and family at Ingomar. We could camp out in Central Park or stay at the Bunk 'n Biscuit.

Note: In spring 2009, the Jersey Lilly was closed. Reportedly the closure is temporary, but it would be best to check ahead before planning a visit.

Montana Bar

612 MAIN STREET, MILES CITY

We drive the forty miles to Forsyth and stop for a spell at a park on the Yellowstone River. I call the Hansons in Miles City. Just my luck they're around and will meet me for dinner before checking out the Montana Bar, one of my favorites. A few hours later we stroll in.

Okay. Let's say it outright. This still is an almost perfect bar.

This is how I described it thirty years ago:

At first glance the Montana appears to be the usual down-on-its-luck old-timer's bar. Its name, printed in unwavering gold across the front door, hints of what lies within. In through the heavy glass door, through the entry of leaded glass and old, shining wood, the first impression of tasteful affluence the Montana breathes is found in its fine inlaid terrazzo floor, an intricate pattern of cut green, yellow, and white marble. The back bar is powerful, towering oak, fitted with a brass foot rail and brass spittoons. Across from the bar sit beautiful square dark-wood booths covered with black horsehide leather. In the center of the stately booths are small oval cherry-wood tables mounted on massive bronze castings that curve with proper neo-Victorian elegance down to the terrazzo marble floor. French-oak ceiling fans revolve lazily. A finely preserved longhorn steer head, mounted above the booths, stares on the furnishings below. A golden light reflects back from the windows, the rich wood, and the smooth, patterned floor.

The cattleman who built the Montana had money, as did the cattle buyers who frequented it. And this bar, not a whole lot different a hundred years after its birth, is a testament to their faith in the cultural and agricultural potential of southeastern Montana.

The Montana's marble floor, stained-glass-and-mahogany entry, soaring three-arch back bar, and massive wood booths have stood the test of time—including death by fire of the building next door. The walk-in cooler still functions, although it no longer is cooled by slabs of ice from the Yellowstone River. The original paddle fans still hang from the embossed tin ceiling. There's also the famed men's room with its marble double-berth urinal.

Deborah and Terry are two of many people who have shepherded the Montana through tough times. After the fire in the mid-1980s, the Montana sat empty for a few years, its west wall deemed compromised by the fire, and the building was marked for demolition. Terry, a Miles City lawyer who had sold newspapers as a kid outside the bar, wasn't about to let that happen. He found a client in Minnesota interested in buying the bar, but the deal fell through at the last minute. Terry says he had just won a lawsuit and had "some cash" so he bought the bar, then gathered together a group of investors, forming a corporation called Watering Hole, Inc. They resurrected the bar in 1989, brought back the beautiful entryway, which for some reason had been put in storage, refinished the back bar, saved the ancient taxidermy of an Audubon bighorn sheep (now extinct) exhibited in the bar's front window, and cleaned up after years of neglect, always with an eye toward historical preservation. The original furnishings were still in such good shape that most just needed a thorough cleaning. Looking proudly around the bar this night, Terry gives one of his pronouncements: "This is a functional museum. Shit—this is it!"

The Hansons ran the place for five years, with Deborah spending a lot of time behind the plank and Terry . . . well, let's just say he called it his living room. In 1994 Deborah wanted to go home so they turned the bar over to another corporation. The new group, Lone Buckaroo, is headed by a Miles City car dealer and managed by Currie Colvin.

The massive gold-plated National cash register that Terry bought for the bar (still on loan to it) is one of many things he is proud of. Another is that Lone Buckaroo has bought the adjacent building, has lined its walls with western art (much of it donated by locals), and has it available for local gatherings. Currie plans to name it the Charlie Brown Room, after one of Miles City's first barmen—the one known for keeping a pot of mulligan stew on twenty-four hours for his customers. Currie is also looking to replace the brass spittoons. Then pretty

☞ An elegant back bar and marble floor display the wealth of the cattleman who built the Montana Bar and the cattle buyers who frequented it one hundred years ago.

CLOSE TO PERFECTION

I wondered when I first walked into the Montana Bar thirty years ago if I had not found a bar about as close to perfect as I was going to find. It was early in my initial bar search, the weekend of the Bucking Horse Sale in late May. Back to Miles City in the fall—twenty classic bars later—my feelings had not changed.

The Montana was established in 1908 by James Kenney. In the late 1870s the first cattle were driven into Montana from Texas. Miles City was the northernmost point on the route. The Montana was built for those early cattlemen who stayed in Montana and parlayed a bull and a handful of heifers into herds that, when trailed, were about half the size of Connecticut.

The booths were meant for business. Cattlemen, and later the sheepherders—the buyers and the sellers—would meet in the Montana to conduct their business. A back room was furnished with chairs and couches, covered like the booths with the black horsehide leather. Reports are that when the men would tire of business, poker, or drink, they'd go in the back room and sleep. The Montana was home off the range.

much all the elements of the original furnishing will be accounted for. There is a pride of history here. Currie was quoted in a *Billings Gazette* article last year: "Nobody really owns it (the bar). We just manage it, like the fair board or something."

Tonight I'm just soaking it all in from a front corner booth, the booth saved for visiting children in the early days. Terry points out bullet holes in the stained-glass entry, saying they used to require that men leave their guns in the entryway and one discharged—an innocent enough offense. "*This is a saloon!*" Terry announces with clear pleasure, again.

Memories wash over me—of finding coolness and quiet on a hot afternoon, of two-stepping with a spry rancher to country music in the back. Of finding haven the morning after a night of Bucking Horse revelry—packing seven people into one of the deep and wide booths—all of us pathetic from closing the bar the night before. In through the back door comes Terry, dressed in a blinding white suit, turquoise dress shirt, and shiny boots. His moustache is curled like the serif of a gothic font and if you didn't know better, you might guess he was back from a long sojourn on a Pacific isle.

Terry, of course, was a main reason we closed the bar, him being the usual rabble-rouser. He tells the story of being called at his office that morning. A man who was becoming known for finding trouble in Miles City got into a fight in another bar the night before. The guy was taken away to the jail and booked. The men he had been in the altercation with waited outside the jail and pounced on the guy when he was released a few hours later, continuing the beating. The guy was then taken to the hospital and eventually made it home. He called Terry, asking him what he should do—should he file a lawsuit, what? Terry told him, "Hell, if I was you, I'd get out of town. Those guys really mean it." He's got us all laughing now. Time for a round of Bloody Marys.

The Hansons greet friends as they come through the door, and Terry tells me how he accumulated some of the mounts on the wall—a pair of oxen look down on us. They had been Miles City staples for years, appearing in parade after parade, Terry says, but they were getting old and lame and it came time to say good-bye. When they were taken to the stockyards, the owner told Terry the two were so tame and trusting they angled their horns to put their heads in the rack. "They were like pets," Terry snorts. And now they're part of the Montana Bar.

The Old Stand

207 Main Street, Ekalaka

It's a two-hour drive to Ekalaka from Miles City. On this rainy day the landscape surprises me with its lonesome beauty. It unfolds in golds and rusts, undulating across eerie expanses, opening up into stream gullies, surging to lone hills and stretching buttes. The colors are subtle, but there are blue-purple rocks and sage and deep-red foliage along creek beds. Water is a definer in these parts. A driver's attention focuses when crossing the Powder River and then O'Fallon Creek. Stands of cottonwood

AT THE END OF THE ROAD

To Montana, Ekalaka is the Town at the End of the Road. For years the state highway led into the southeastern corner of the state to Ekalaka but not an inch past. Eventually the state paved the road for eighteen miles past Ekalaka; then it turns to gravel. But a few more miles of paved road hasn't lessened Ekalaka's reputation as a dead-end town. That's why it is ironic that in Montana's early days, the road started at Ekalaka.

Around 1882 Claude Carter, a buffalo hunter and saloon keeper, was traveling west into Montana with a wagon full of logs that he was going to use to build a saloon to cater to the cowboys who worked on the huge cattle ranches that had spread from Texas to South Dakota, spilling over into Montana Territory. His horses balked in muddy ground. Russell got down from the wagon, spit on the ground, and said, "Hell, any place in Montana is a good place to build a saloon." He threw the logs off the wagon and proceeded to do just that. When he was done, he named it the Old Stand. Ekalaka grew up around the saloon and was named for the first woman settler, an Ogalala Sioux, the wife of rancher David Russell.

The way the crow flies, it's about eighty miles from Forsyth, where I started my day thirty years ago, to Ekalaka, a short jaunt in that unpopulated corner of the state. The way the road goes, it's more like 180 miles. Ekalakians are an hour from Baker, a good two hours from Miles City, and five hours from a town that could qualify as a city—a town of a thousand people at best, on the road to nowhere.

A person doesn't just "pass through" Ekalaka, I thought as I sipped my beer, feeling like an outsider at the Old Stand. The usual response to "What y'all doin' in Dodge?" —"Just passin' through"—simply would not work.

The bartender didn't know quite what to do with me. I was the only woman in the bar—and a young, unattached stranger at that. Finally he sauntered over and we talked a little about the end of the road. "Yeah," he said, "we get left out of a lot of things. Maybe it's for the best."

Old cowboys sat at the end of the long bar, greeting each other cordially. They drank beer only from a glass and rolled their own cigarettes. Interest perked when I got the camera out and began to shoot a few frames of the bar and the old cowboys. In other towns a camera can kill all possibilities of a good conversation. In Ekalaka it proved to be an opening. A couple of the men told me to talk to Ernie, one of the old guys at the end of the bar. Ernie heard and sat up a little closer to the bar for the picture.

Ernie was a convivial, weather-beaten, barrel-chested, throaty old man. A worn black Stetson pushed to the back of his head framed a face at one minute dead-pan serious, the next breaking into jigsaw puzzle lines with his cigarette hack of a laugh. A crowd gathered to egg Ernie on. "Tell her the sister-in-law story," one guy said. Chuckles from the group. "Ah, naw," said Ernie, "not that one."

"All right, then tell her about stealing the horses." Ernie served a little time after he was caught trucking another man's horses from some point in South Dakota. Getting caught didn't bother him much, according to Ernie. Just another day's work. I asked him why he did it. The answer was something like "Because they were there."

Then there's the story about how cattle rustlers would butcher their take and throw the head and hooves down a well; the one about how he burnt down the bar of a guy who was his only competition in Alzada; and the one about how he once sold a dude quarts of Black Roses (whisky brewed from potatoes) claiming it was the best he had, and charging accordingly.

This Ernie appeared to be quite the scoundrel. But the old cowboys kept asking for the sister-in-law story, the one Ernie wouldn't tell. Ernie mentioned he'd been married nine times. "I couldn't keep a woman. I'd usually get 'em in the fall and lose 'em in the spring. Then I'd have to get another one." A few of the guys won't buy it that Ernie's been married only nine times. Ernie's only child from all those unions runs the Old Stand. He passed by and a guy asked, "Hey, Sam, how many times Ernie been married?"

(continued on page 108)

(continued from page 107)

"Nine," Ernie reiterated. "Hell," said Sam, "you've been married twelve or thirteen times." Gales of laughter from the crowd. Tell her the sister-in-law story. Naw, said Ernie, not that one. "You ought to stay for the wedding dance," Ernie told me. "It'll be a good one." I'd had several beers bought for me by this time, and staying overnight was tempting. A wedding dance in Ekalaka would be an occasion that would live on in memory. And who could say when I'd be in Ekalaka again. (Being in Ekalaka, to me, is still something like being in another country. Its removal alone makes it precious.) Naw, I have to go, I said. They're expecting me back in Forsyth.

Ernie's current wife came in. A pleasant middle-aged woman, she was a nursing student in Miles City and commuted to Ekalaka on weekends. Ernie transformed from the rollicking scoundrel to the righteous, gentle husband. He invited me to stay at their place overnight. It was hard to say no. I gathered my things and started for the door. As I left, the man who had led the laughter is the fourth person to say to me—in these same words—"Sure hate to see ya go."

trees and pines in the distance mark creeks and springs.

When I get to Ekalaka, I'm 630 miles and four days from my home in Missoula. I haven't been here since my first book came out, but I have fond memories of the Old Stand. So I'm a little shocked when I walk in the door and find an almost new interior. Nothing is the same. My first thought is of the Dirty Shame in the Yaak. It, too, has changed beyond recognition. It's interesting that these two community stalwarts in the remotest corners of the state are the ones that have changed the most.

Today the Old Stand is a clean and wholesome community-oriented lounge, a far cry from the worn cowboy parlor I visited before. I take up a stool and order a draft. A banner outside welcomes hunters, but the only clientele around noon are two high-school girls shooting pool, a girl bartender who looks too young to drink, and two women sitting across from me at the pretty U-shaped bar. It takes me a while to understand the Old Stand I knew is really gone. I learn later that it burned years before.

After a few minutes of me watching them and them trying not to watch me, I offer a comment: "I don't know if I've ever been in a bar with just women in it." That gets a laugh and breaks the ice. One of them says, "I like to come here when it's quiet." It's rather funny because when I was here before, I was the only woman in the bar amid a sea of locals and cowboys.

Pretty soon the owner of the bar, Skeet Hedges, comes in. He remembers me from the last time I visited. The Old Stand has been in the Hedges family off and on since 1932. Skeet and I chat a little; he tells me the local economy is picking up a little. "We're even getting a few of those damn Californians," he says with a laugh.

Hotel Howdy Bar
807 Main Street, Forsyth

The red letters beckon travelers to Forsyth. HOTEL HOWDY they shout out from the roof of the tallest building in town. Many travelers know Forsyth exists solely because the Howdy calls out to them.

The Howdy's been around for ages and is now listed on the National Register of Historic Buildings. It was built over three years, pretty much by one man—Hiram Marceyes—to serve railroaders and rail passengers. Marceyes started in 1903 and finished the decorative brickwork of the three-story building in 1906.

The architecture was Renaissance Revival. He named it the Commercial Hotel, and it was a success. Indeed, conductors would call out the name of the hotel as they neared Forsyth, not the name of the town. In the 1950s it was renamed the Howdy to cash in on a western theme and as such represents the ranching/farming/railroad town of my birth.

The Howdy has been owned and operated for more than a hundred years by Marceyes and his descendants. The latest owners are Jan (Dean) and Max Bauer. Jan is the daughter of Esther and Walter Dean Jr., the grandson of Marceyes and son of Walter Dean, storekeeper and noted photographer of early-day Rosebud County. I grew up across the street from the Deans. Walter, known to everyone as Junior Dean, ran it then, and there was always talk about the Howdy. His son, Gordon, was my best friend from about age two to seven, and one of our favorite things to do was jump on Junior from the top of his four-poster bed every day around noon to wake him up. Junior was a character—a jazz musician, uranium prospector, lawyer, inheritor of the Marceyes estate, a sort of second father, so different from my own. But that's another story.

Driving west from Miles City, I stop in Forsyth and visit several local haunts of my youth. I take Bailey for a walk at one of my favorite spots on the Yellowstone and drive by many buildings in town that have been placed on the Historical Register. Slowly it dawns on me that the Howdy Bar might be worth a stop. I never ventured into the bar as a kid. It was known then as kind of a rough, grown-up sort of place.

I pull up a stool and soak in the ambience of a bar that's had a parallel life to mine, but a bar I've never met. A fading mural of an Old West scene—cowboys, cattle, sagebrush, open vistas—stretches across the wall opposite the back bar, a solid, clean art deco, no doubt a part of many remodeling projects over the years. The floor is black-and-white tile. A fine replica of a model train stretches across the top of the bar. Names and brands carved into the wood crowd one another on a pine bar rail. I learn that food is available from the Speedway Diner next door. A young man comes in and joins two middle-aged women who are chatting at the bar. He notes he's in town because after a soaking rain the day before, "it's still too wet to farm." I have a draft beer for $1.25 and think about my childhood.

Many characters—noteworthy, sad, inspiring, self-defeating, talented, heroic, paranoid, small-minded, cantankerous, comical, tragic—almost all of them hard-working—march through my mind. I am the child of a railroad/ranching town that grew on the banks of the Yellowstone River. There are many such towns in southeastern Montana. Our roots are still clearly visible and live on in places like the Howdy.

The Rex Hotel
2401 MONTANA AVENUE, BILLINGS

I had asked the Hansons in Miles City what bars in Billings might be worth a stop. They regularly make the drive west to Missoula and have been bar hoppers for years, so I value their opinion. Deborah has a hard time at first. We talk about the cowboy bar, the Seventeen, which I wrote about before; it's gone. An hour later, Deborah, having thought about it and consulted with friends, tells me I should stop in at the Rex.

So this Monday afternoon I wander in, very ready at half past two for lunch. The Rex, built as a hotel in 1910 and restored in the 1980s after being saved in 1975 from the wrecking ball, is a very nice place. Its island bar, with Indian pictographs from local caves etched into a concrete surface, handsome oak booths, tin ceiling, tile floors, brass fixtures, and stained and beveled glass give

SONNY O'DAY'S BAR & LOUNGE

Coming back from Red Lodge thirty years ago, I was about to take the interstate ramp to Billings when a bar mentioned by people in my travels surfaces in my mind. Sonny something, I thought, yeah and he's in Laurel.

A few minutes later, I opened the door to Sonny O'Day's. I was greeted promptly, aggressively. His speech was unmistakably Butte—Brooklyn once removed. "Where's your old man?" was the first thing. "Don't have one," was the reply. That bothered him. "Where ya from?" Almost before I replied he asked, "Who's your family?" I told him. He was delighted. He knew my father.

Then I remembered. Sonny O'Day was the boxer who ran a bar in Laurel and was a stronghold in eastern Montana Democratic politics. A look around told the story: Democrats and boxers all over the place and a painting of Sonny in younger days standing by the Savoy in what was once Meaderville, Butte.

At the end of the bar a life-size photo of Sonny in boxing shorts was stretched from ceiling to below bar level. It was probably taken before his twenty-first birthday. It was a photo of a beautiful, smooth-bodied, strong-faced young man bent gracefully at the waist, a determined glare on his face, dukes up for the camera.

I began the usual bombardment of questions, but Sonny had a mile lead. (An article that appeared in the *Billings Gazette* mentioned his rapid speech, and others I talked to later about Sonny were quick to laugh about how fast he talked.)

Sonny took my hand and led me around his establishment, what he called a boxing museum. Calling me "darlink" and "babee" and swooping up my hand should he lose it as he darted from here to there, he showed me his collection of photos and with that breathless speech, told the story behind each. He claimed to have photos of a thousand fighters, all of them personally autographed; sixty-seven world champions, eleven of them in photographs with Sonny behind the bar.

(continued on page 112)

(continued from page 111)

There's Rocky Marciano, Floyd Patterson, and a photo of the first legal fight on the Pacific Coast, at Colma, California, in 1905. There's Mose LaFonsie and the original Dixie Kid—bare knuckles in Boulder, Montana, twenty-five rounds. There's "Sugar" Ray Robinson, Sonny Liston, and Sonny's prize promotion, a middleweight championship fight between Joey Giardello and Gene Fulmer in Bozeman in 1960. Sonny called it a draw.

There were Butte boxers—the Michigan Assassin and Montana Jack Sullivan. Five world champions lived in Butte shortly after the turn of the century, Sonny said. There's John L. "Slug 'Em" Sullivan and Primo Carnera. There's Jack Dempsey tending bar with Sonny.

One of my favorites hung behind the bar—Charlie Russell posed with Jack Dempsey. And there was Cassius Clay sitting in what was once a training room, now opened up and part of the bar. Sonny said his bar was nationally famous as a boxing museum, a home of champions.

But more interesting than all the photos on his wall was Sonny himself. What was a guy so obviously Butte doing in Laurel? Sonny took me around the story a few different routes over the hours I spent with him. Here's the gist: forget the Irish of his name. Sonny is as Italian as fettuccine. Charles George was his given name. He was ten years old, a punk in Butte with a paper route, when promoters spotted him in an altercation. Shortly thereafter, he fought in the hundred-pound division in a boxing-crazed Butte.

The promoters gave him a new name, so his father—recovering from a World War I wound in Fort Harrison—wouldn't know his son was boxing. They spelled it Sunny O'Dea.

A few years later, Sonny's father was still ailing and wanted to return to his birthplace, Lucca, Italy. Sonny accompanied him to Italy. From there he boxed in North Africa, Hungary, Italy, and Spain.

"I was an orphan at fourteen years of age," Sonny told me. "I had to fight to live." By the time he was sixteen, he was a professional boxer, a ham-n-egger, a welterweight. His strength was in his left. Only the managers made money in those days, Sonny told me. His manager was a gambler. Sonny fought 529 fights and retired to Butte in 1938. He got a job as a bouncer at a place called the Rocky Mountain Cafe in Meaderville. Then he bought into the Savoy, one of Meaderville's choice joints, as he described it. "One a da girlie joints, ya know—bootleggin, back in da turdies, in da Depression."

He began to build what he called a financial empire. Then came World War II. Sonny was gone for six years, and when he returned to Butte he found his financial empire had dribbled to nothing. He lost the Savoy and another bar he owned—the Melody Lane—burned to the ground.

With the usual Butte-bred irony, Sonny said, "Dat town cost me two-hundret and seventy-seven tousant dollars—it took everting I had." The next minute he was calling Butte his town. A few minutes later he called it the Sacred City, the last title I would have expected for Butte. "Why?" I asked. "Tree Catholic bishops" were born in Butte, he said, "dat's why."

Sonny landed in Billings, where he worked in a bar for a time. Then the bar owner set him up with the place in Laurel. Sonny made a good living at the bar, but to hear him talk, it was only a sideline to his ongoing boxing career. He was still on the state's boxing commission (an appointed position, no doubt a good part of the reason for all the politicians' photos in the bar) and was working on a book on boxing. He said he stayed on top of the sport that he called with reverence "the manly art of self-defense." Today he was taking the bus to Butte to check up on a fight he suspected was not entirely aboveboard.

I had to get back on the road, too, but first I asked if I could take his picture. Sure, he said. Out in front of his bar, an opulent October sun drenching us in its descent, Sonny made me pose with him in the same stance so many politicians and fighters assume—legs angled, about eighteen inches apart, knuckles tight, dukes up—hold for the camera. Sonny positioned his dukes so he had the inside with his famous left. Then he enlisted an old man passing by to take the photo.

A few minutes later I was on my way out the door of the bar again. Sonny said, "Here, take a few beers wid ya." "Nah," I said, "that's okay." "Oh yeah," he said. "Well, maybe one for the road," I said. Sonny got back behind the bar. He grabbed a grocery bag and started filling it with beer, potato chips, gum, candy, popcorn, pretzels, beer nuts. When I protested, he said, "You're on da road, ain't ya?" A few minutes later I was walking out the door looking like I just did a week's shopping.

But Sonny was still worried I didn't have enough to eat. He asked me if I liked Reese's candy bars. I'd seen him throw at least three Reese's into the sack, so I told him, sure, thinking that would please him. He ran back and got me a couple more. "Reese's are good for ya, ya know—dere not fattening."

He walked me to the Renault, talking about his birthplace. He was planning a trip to Lucca, Italy. A minute later we were driving over to his house to see a book on Lucca. There he gave me a sack of Macintosh apples.

Note: Sonny O'Day's was shut up tight when Sonny died in 2001. One of his daughters holds the liquor license, so there is hope it will reopen in the future.

it a historical feel, even if it's a newly remodeled historical feel. The remodeling efforts of the famed hotel built by Buffalo Bill Cody's chef Alfred Heimer were good enough to win an award for renovation of a historic building.

The Rex, once a hotel that catered to the likes of Cody, Calamity Jane, and Will James, was also known as the Buffalo Bill Bar and locally advertised as a place with "cold beer and good German lunches." Little of that is left today, but what it's been replaced with—a main bar, airy and open, with excellent furnishings; a piano bar that serves as the entrance to a heralded restaurant; and a handsome patio grill area—are the center of a renovation of historic Montana Avenue and as such are as noteworthy today as Heimer's endeavor a hundred years ago. Besides, I like the idea of drinking where Calamity Jane drank. And the roasted red pepper soup, crusty bread, and Caesar salad are delicious.

Stacey's Old Faithful Bar & Steakhouse

300 MILL STREET, GALLATIN GATEWAY

There's something about roadhouse bars that I find uniquely compelling. Emigrant's Old Saloon would be in that category, as well as the Jersey Lilly in Ingomar, the Blue Moon in Columbia Falls, and the Northern Lights in Polebridge. Food is an important part of the deal, and they often are destinations in themselves. Stacey's Old Faithful fits right in with this hall of champions.

Pulling up outside the handsome two-story circa 1912 brick building, I take in the two plate-glass windows and doors on each side that give it a pleasing openness and symmetry. I learn later that the building, like many havens for today's old saloons, originally had many other functions, housing over the years a butcher shop, telephone office, and clothing store. In the 1920s, after Montana repealed Prohibition, the legendary Mae Ping created a saloon here with "apartments" upstairs.

I didn't include Stacey's in my first book. Indeed, I didn't know about it until reading an article by Toby Thompson, a fine writer who also penned a bar book—one spanning the country's great bars—called *Saloon*. He'd missed Stacey's, too. So I don't feel too bad, but I'm happy today to put my ignorance to rest.

I've been driving for days, and it feels good to pull up a worn bar stool as the crystalline midday light of the Gallatin Valley pours in the front window. The bartender is a pretty young brunette named Wendy. She fits right in, with her Levis, silver belt buckle, and boots. Quickly approaching a regular—an older rancher by the looks of him—Wendy announces, "You've got six beers coming."

The man is a little slow to reply as he considers his lunch options. She brings him a beer. "I knew I had fun that night," the guy finally says. "But I didn't know I had that much fun."

I walk around the bar, which reminds me of an old-time cluttered living room. There are wonderful black-and-white photos of all sorts of rodeoers, mainly guys riding bucking horses and bulls, hung on wood-plank walls. A worn piano with an oil painting of a classic Montana scene stretching above it commands attention along one wall. There are mismatched bar tables and stools that get pushed out of the way for music and dancing on Friday and Saturday nights.

Photos of Stacey Crosby and his wife, Phyllis, who bought the bar from Mae Ping in 1963, take up much of one wall. There are several of Stacey and/or Phyllis posed inside the bar with a Brahma bull, Buford T. Light, the official mascot for Miller Light. The back bar is mainly mirrors, but the old cherrywood cabinets under it are handsome, 1940s vintage.

A pretty side room, the steak house, features shiny handmade pine furniture and more historical photos. In 2004 the Crosbys' daughter, Toni Donnelly, divided the bar straight down the middle, putting the steak house on one side. On the wall between the two is the bar's signature photo of a bison, catapulting several feet from an upraised area into a pool of water. It is a stunning photo that raises questions, obviously, in the viewer's mind. Later I'll learn from Toni that that was something they did for fun back around the turn of the twentieth century. They'd launch the bison into a pool of water, where people straddled their backs as they swam around. "It looks inhumane in a way," Toni says, "but it really didn't hurt the buffalo."

Her dad Stacey, a character by all accounts, was known for his propensity for a beer or two and for sheltering rodeo riders and U.S. veterans. "My Dad had a soft spot for veterans," Toni tells me. "They got free drinks all night."

Stacey rode bulls as a young man, but broke his elbow, ending his rodeo career. So he bought a bar and made it a haven for rodeo cowboys. Toni says they'd come from all over, often sleeping on the pool table at night or on the floor of the family apartment upstairs. "We'd wake up and find cowboys asleep all over the place," she remembers.

When her dad first bought the bar, Toni announced to her kindergarten class that they should come to the Old Faithful. "Drinks are on the house," she said. Like most children, the girls sometimes tired of their parents' long work hours. They'd take it out on bar patrons by leaning out a front window and shooting BBs into people's butts as they left the bar. "They'd jump like chickens," she says and laughs. Other times she'd lean out the window and tell people the bar was closed when it wasn't.

She rode her horse into the place many times. "I'd ride in and Mae would give me candy bars and a pop." The Old Faithful is still open to livestock when the cause is right. A man dressed as Juan Valdez for the Halloween party brought his mule in with him. "He [the mule] sat by the jukebox all night," Toni remembers. "He was part of the costume."

Toni, who left her career as an emergency room nurse in Seattle in 2003 to take over the bar after her mother died, is a storyteller, cut from the same cloth as her father. Photos of her parents, married in 1948, reveal a beautiful couple—as attractive as any people on earth. But they definitely were opposites. Stacey was a gregarious hard-living cowboy, a Butte kid orphaned as a child,

bartender at the age of seventeen; her mother a strait-laced Mormon girl who threatened to divorce Stacey many times. She says many people in Gallatin Gateway early on thought her mother might be simple because she would just nod at people and smile, not quite knowing what to do with the local cowboys and the motley crew Stacey attracted. But Phyllis was the backbone of the place, the quiet center in the storm.

One story Toni clearly likes to tell is when a lawyer delivered divorce papers to her dad at the bar. He crumpled them up and threw them on the bar plank. Later, he thought better of it and spread the papers out on the bar. A few minutes later he admitted, "It's going to take Perry Mason to get me out of this one."

One guy named Archie would often sleep on a couch Stacey had in the bar. One morning they came in to find him pinned on top of the piano, with their two German shepherds patrolling below. He had been up there all night and was terrified. Toni tells a story of how Mae would deal with fights by turning off the lights, thinking "there's no glory in the dark," but that reasoning was proved faulty one night when the lights came back on to show the piano player's throat had been slit. Mae would never admit to having prostitutes upstairs, but Toni says tokens that have been brought into the bar may have been used for women's services. Mae always said she rented the rooms to the girls and "what they did up there was between them, God, and the IRS."

Toni tells me she does miss her life as an ER nurse, but it became clear when her mother died that it was her parents' plan that she have the bar. Her sisters, Marti and Cody, still live in the area and have pitched in to keep the Old Faithful running. But Toni's the proprietor and keeps the place lively much the same way her father did. She's a little disappointed there aren't as many fights in the bar as there used to be. "I miss all the blood and guts from the emergency room," she sighs. But there are no plans to sell the place. "How can you sell something that's been in the family for years?" she asks. A good question.

10

LEWISTOWN
AND CENTRAL MONTANA

With not much more than a month to complete my travels, Thanksgiving weekend is designated for bar research. I've enlisted Kelly and Bailey for companionship, and we're off early Thursday morning. We plan to take advantage of a small-town Montana custom—providing a Thanksgiving Day dinner to patrons in the town saloon. Martinsdale happens to be on the bar path this weekend and I've learned the Mint is open, so that is our first stop.

The Mint

107 MAIN STREET, MARTINSDALE

Sure enough, a few steps in the door and a woman invites us to dish up from a broad buffet in the back. We get a couple of beers and sit down with a tasty dinner. I note a pretty cherrywood back bar similar to the one in Ingomar's Jersey Lilly. A lineup of some twenty mule

deer heads with five-point racks—all shot in 1943 or 1944—stretches along the wall. A historical plaque outside says the building was erected in 1938. A sign on the door makes it plain what animals will not be allowed in the bar: dogs, cats, badgers, cows, snakes, and any other creatures.

Hunters and locals are lined up at the plank. I talk with Sheila, who is the source of all good things today. Although it was advertised as a potluck, only Sheila and the bartender, Norma, brought any food. But there's plenty of it and quite an assortment of dishes. Sheila cooked most of it, starting at five in the morning. She's visiting from Rawlins, Wyoming. Many locals help her mother, who can't drive because of legal problems, Sheila says, so she comes back occasionally and cooks up a storm as a payback. She says the absentee owner

☞ Gamblers play with big bucks at the Mint in Martinsdale.

of the bar wanted to close for the day, but Sheila and her mother believe in taking care of the bachelors and other locals who could use a Thanksgiving dinner. It's clear all of these small-town bars rely on this sort of generosity, which usually hangs on a thread of a few giving people.

A couple days later I'll be disappointed to find the Two Dot Bar closed. It's for sale and wasn't open when we came through on a Saturday. Locals said you can't count on them opening when they say they will—that you should knock on the door to get them to open up. We decide any bar we have to push our way into isn't worth putting in the book, but by the time this comes out, the Two Dot may have new owners, so count it down but not out.

The Midway

416 West Main, Lewistown

Another disappointment comes the next day when I walk into the Midway. It's become a full-fledged casino. I had been afraid this would happen—one of the bars from the earlier book would go over to the dark side. I've visited some fifty or sixty saloons and this is the first time I've been confronted with my early fear—that I would find the Montana bar had lost all semblance of its past because of those damned machines. I suppose that makes me lucky. There have been poker and keno machines in most of the bars I've visited, but they've usually been shuffled to the side or a back room or integrated into the action of the bar in a way that

does nothing to threaten the general ambience and conversational center of the place.

The Midway is all machines today, although the handsome art deco oak back bar can still be found in the back of the long room. But there aren't any bar stools, which reminds me of the old days before stools were introduced in saloons. This time, however, it's to ensure no one gets too comfortable at a place where gambling dollars can't be raked in. I stand at the bar and order a bourbon on the rocks. It's barely noon, but it's cold and windy outside and I need to calm down.

It's not that I dislike gambling. I love a good black-jack or poker game in a place where wit, reflexes, and an ability to bluff or remember cards contributes to success. I just loathe the mindless diddling that happens on these machines. And the odds. And the fact that they substitute for social interaction. And that they've taken over a perfectly good bar.

The bartender feels for me when I tell her why I'm here. She says I should stop at the Montana Tavern. She says they have a window that looks below the bar into Spring Creek and she talks animatedly about seeing the same fish in the creek every time she goes into the bar.

Montana Tavern

202 West Main Street, Lewistown

Indeed, you can look through the floor to Spring Creek, which runs beneath the bar. I see some sort of fish feeding down there, maybe a trout, maybe a sucker.

This is unique in my travels and is definitely worth a stop in Lewistown if you enjoy seeing fish swimming in the raw.

I take up a bar stool in the sprawling expanse that includes a few pool tables and many poker and keno machines back to back, positioned like they do in Vegas, with an awning over the top. Now I'm in the mood for vodka so I have a Citron on the rocks. Somehow today I need the hard stuff. There are a few people at the bar, but it's so long as to present quite a distance between stools. It's not long before the young bartender leaves her position behind the bar and goes across the room to plug money into a poker machine. This is a new one. I've never seen a bartender leave her post to play a machine.

Soon I leave my post as well, giving up on the bars in Lewistown.

Willow Creek Cafe and Saloon

21 MAIN STREET, WILLOW CREEK

I first heard of this place when reading a story in *True West* magazine. Two writers had a little repartee on the best saloons in the West. The only one mentioned in this list of ten from Montana was the Willow Creek Saloon, and the reason for that was that it served oysters on the half shell. Imagine my chagrin when I realized I knew nothing of the place. This will be rectified at the end of the Thanksgiving weekend. It's our last planned stop.

We arrive, hungry for lunch at about three in the afternoon. I really don't know what to expect but I'm pleased to spot the sign on the two-story yellow wood building as the road from Three Forks angles onto Willow Creek's main street. We park on the side of the building near an exhaust fan; the aroma of all things good greets us as we open the truck door. A short walk for Bailey and then up onto the front porch.

A step in the door creates a pleasing sensation for me—the ambience is turn-of-the-nineteenth-century mercantile—high ceilings, flowered wallpaper, a small but stately back bar at the end of one room, chandeliers and old oak tables and chairs creating a dining room in another, artwork by locals on the walls, farm antiques making their own statements here and there, gas fireplaces warming both rooms, and a unique elk mount, the elk caught forever in a bugling call, its head angled to the side, yearning to give the sound full amplitude. No poker or keno machines. Anywhere.

We pull up a table in the bar area and order lunch and a couple of beers. I wander around a little, looking at the artwork, reading framed stories about the cafe and saloon, noting the large number of people in the place in mid-afternoon on a Sunday. I've ordered a farmer's Rueben—made with pork and sauerkraut with a sweet cheese melted on top—and butternut squash soup. Kelly gets the burger and fries. All very yummy. Too bad we're too early for dinner. I move on up to the bar and order another Mirror Pond Ale on tap. It's clear this is a classy joint. They have three beers on tap—Beltian White, Copper John Scotch Ale, and Mirror Pond. I see the front bar is gleaming oak made by Rothschild's and Sons, 739 and

THE OLD MIDWAY

The Midway was small, clean, orderly, and dark in midday on my first visit, with a fine old dark-wood back bar inlaid with mirrors and stained glass. To the side of the bar was a Chinese restaurant. Tony Geis, who owned the Midway then, also sold takeout liquor, basic grocery items, and assorted merchandise including wood-burning stoves. I learned a lot about the bankrolling of ranch hands and sheepherders from Tony. He talked to me about the old days, when the hands would come in from the range: "They'd come in and cash a check. Then the bartender would parcel it out in twenties and fifties. The first thing they'd do is get a shave and a haircut. Then they'd go to Jason's and get a hat and a pair of boots. They'd always come in with a bedroll. In the case of a sheepherder, you always had their dog. The dog would lie down under a table. Generally the boss knew how long it would take for them to spend their money."

Tony assured me Lena Ford was a main bankroller in Great Falls, adding it was her practice to fill a whiskey bottle with tea so she could drink all day with the boys. Tony remembered another bankrolling instance in a bar in Harlem: "A sheepherder drove up to this house and had $600. He was buying all the drinks. Everyone crowded around. A rancher came in and took the madam into the kitchen. He told her he definitely had to have the sheepherder back by Saturday—to make sure the guy's money was gone by then. You could tell those guys they were broke in three days and they'd never know it."

Tony spent most of his life in a bar. During Prohibition he watched his father bootleg whiskey. He remembered when his father stored 150 cases of whiskey. "He said he had enough to last the rest of this life," Tony said. "It was gone in three years."

Like Charley and Esther Judd, Sonny O'Day, Moose, Luigi, Trixi, and so many of the bartenders I met on my first search, Tony Geis was a pro. These people were respected and revered as modern-day storytellers, entertainers, and purveyors of local legend, as well as important contemporary information sources. If you wanted to know something about an area, likely you would be sent to one of these men or women.

You rarely would see them take a drink. Most of them would sit and drink coffee and tell you stories for about as long as you could listen. You would see every sort of person in their bars. And you would see them treat these very different people with equal respect and hospitality. You rarely saw any trouble in their bars. If there was a fight, their customers would usually take care of the disturbance. They were astute business people and they'd try to sell you anything. Take Tony Geis—with his shrimp, fried rice, and eggrolls, his wood-burning stoves, imported olives, and take-out wine.

Tony grew up in Great Falls. He talked about playing with Charlie Russell's stepson as a young boy: "I used to beat up the stepson. Then one of us would cry and [Russell] would call us into the cabin where they lived, and he'd talk to us, and then hand us a horse or a cow that he'd formed out of clay while he was talking to us."

741 Broadway. The matching back bar is art deco, very stylish. Pheasant mounts are perched on top. A worker is cleaning the chandeliers that hang on each side. Locals are chatting on both sides of me at the short bar, placing their orders for dinner, although they're told they won't get them until after five. I ask the friendly young woman next to me if she lives near here. Indeed, she is one of a couple hundred people who call Willow Creek home. She tells me the building has housed a mercantile, dance hall, brothel, and cafe over the years. It's always been the community gathering spot. Our waitress notes her grandfather used to fiddle for dances upstairs. Today Tim Andrescick, one of the two chefs that bought the place in 1991, lives upstairs.

Andrescick and Deane Mitchell between them have a long resumé as chefs and there's a few newspaper articles framed around the place extolling their cuisine, notably their ribs with a mustard glaze. I think it appropriate that they sometimes offer oysters on the half shell; oysters were among the fancy foods that arrived early on in the western saloon. Teddy Blue in *We Pointed Them North* wrote in the 1880s: "Do you know what was the first thing a cowpuncher ordered to eat when he got to town? Oysters and celery. And eggs. Those things were what he didn't get and what he was crazy for."

A couple come in with a young boy. It seems the woman has just shot a deer and they have it out in the truck. The woman next to me buys them a drink and is excited when she hears about the deer. Soon, they're all out the door to check it out.

"It's about time for us to end this three-day adventure," Kelly says as he comes in from checking on Bailey. I finish my beer, seeing a sign at the end of the bar that's more a prayer than anything: LORD HELP ME TO BE THE PERSON MY DOG THINKS I AM.

Owned by two chefs, the Willow Creek Cafe and Saloon is known for culinary specialties such as oysters on the half shell and ribs with mustard glaze.

11

MISSOULA

issoula has always been a great bar-hopping town. In my youth, you could traverse six blocks of downtown—from Front Street to Alder Street—without having to walk much at all on the street. You could start at the Stockman's, cross to the Top Hat, go through the back alley to the back of the Flame (gone) or the Missoula Club, cross the street to the Turf on Broadway (burned down), head through a parking lot to the back door of the Oxford, cross the street to Connie's (now Sean Kelly's), cross Spruce and enter through the back door of Al & Vic's, then cross Alder Street to the Park Hotel (long gone).

One Friday night in January 2009, Kelly, friends Dianne and Dave, and I set out on another Missoula pub crawl—from Al & Vic's to the Oxford, with many stops in between. Unfortunately, in 2009 the route includes few alleys. Conditions are typical for this time of year—cold and icy.

Al & Vic's

119 WEST ALDER STREET, MISSOULA

Al & Vic's has always been known for its stiff drinks. If you don't ask for a single at this bar, you automatically get a double. It's an old-time saloon; in fact, the regulars will tell you that it is the oldest bar still in its original spot in Missoula. (The Oxford, the oldest running bar in town, changed locations in 1955.) Kelly goes to the bar and brings back a double gin and tonic for me in a pint-size glass and a beer for himself.

This clearly is a college hangout at night. I note the HOME FREE MISSOULA sign (taxi rides for those who have consumed too much to drive) and a photo of what looks to be a seventy-year-old bearded miner with the caption underneath "If you don't look this old, I need to see a picture I.D."

But Al & Vic's has a much broader appeal. You'll see about any age group in the bar most nights, and the days have always been given over to the older crowd. Historical black-and-white photos of Missoula line one wall, along with photos of softball teams, with the bar's slogan "Where the Elite Meet" written on the pictures. Later I will talk with owner Vicky Hammond and ask her where the slogan came from.

She tells me her husband, Mike, who she bought the bar with in 1991, took care of a group of elderly people who lived across the street in upstairs apartments and other spots downtown. They'd come to Al & Vic's every morning at eight. Mike cashed their Social Security checks and helped them navigate the system. For some, he'd divvy up the check and put it in four envelopes, giving out an envelope a week so they were sure to have enough money to last the month. For a few the bar was their permanent address. "There would be eighteen people lined up to get in at eight a.m.," Vicky tells me—what Mike dubbed the "Elite." Now Mike and the Elite are gone, the last of the group dying last year. So Al & Vic's opens at ten in the morning instead of eight.

Vicky tells me that Al and Vic Pepe's father bought the bar for them in 1936; Al ran it alone for a while, and was joined by Vic after World War II. The Pepes had it until the late 1980s. It's a Missoula institution, a quiet working man's bar with little pretense, a haven from the storm.

A few years ago Vicky and her current husband financed her son's interest in another sort of venue, a rather new animal to the Missoula bar scene, the James Bar, an architecturally pleasing, open, and rambling space that connects to Al & Vic's through a side door. The James' theme is counterculture, rock and roll, urban chic. I like the architecture of stone, wood, and mirrors, the open fireplace with gas flames feeding into smooth stones, the outlaw quotes on the walls and the massive black-and-white photos of Janis Joplin and Keith Richards. Outside a quote from Hunter Thompson is etched in stone. I've enjoyed the place the few times I've been in. This is my generation they're immortalizing after all. It's interesting that the James' clientele leans more toward the thirty-something crowd. They do have some very good bar food. Tonight I eat a couple of sliders brought over from the James, to fortify myself for the evening. Then it's on to Charlie's.

Charlie B's
428 NORTH HIGGINS AVENUE, MISSOULA

Charlie B's is the only bar I know that doesn't have a sign out front. Charlie Baumgartner is known for his soft spot and that's the reason he took the sign down, along with the neon lights in the bar's front windows. Charlie has long been known as someone who takes care of people. He rents two stories of apartments upstairs to people who live on fixed incomes and he's often hired or sheltered people down on their luck. Then there are big feeds for both Thanksgiving and Christmas for anyone who wants to come, and God knows how many other acts of charity. But there has to be a limit. He'll tell me later that he took the sign down because of the transients it would attract.

Of course, you won't find Charlie B's listed in the phone book either. If you want to know the address, you might look to a slogan coined years ago by a regular: "On the corner of Space and Time." Of course, Charlie B's is not on a corner, at least not a literal corner. But it can be spacey and it's definitely timeless.

The four of us walk into the bar around eight at night and it's packed as usual. Somehow we wrangle seats at the bar, a half-moon affair that allows people at one end to be able to see down the line. This is when the stories start. We all have stories about Charlie's and other bars. We're fairly new friends, and the stories are new, so this will add to the revelry of the night. Dianne will tell us about the bar her great-grandfather owned south of Philipsburg in the 1920s, Porter's Corner. At the time people were mapping the roads in Montana, and Porter offered them free drinks if they'd put his bar on the map. It obviously worked. Later her great-grandfather had to shoot a man who was threatening others in his bar, but as soon as he shot him, he loaded the guy up in a car and got him to a hospital. The man didn't make it and Porter was tried, but acquitted. Today the bar is long gone but Porter's Corner still exists on Montana maps.

I look around the bar and contemplate the black-and-white photos of Missoula barflies taken by famed photographer Lee Nye over the years. They give the place a depth, a haunting sort of history. Many of the larger photos were taken in the alley behind the bar in the 1960s and 1970s and were hung in Eddy's Club, the first bar in this location.

Charlie bought the place in 1980 and spent several years gathering the photos—probably a hundred or more—the smaller ones from Connie's Lounge and the larger ones bought from Doug Curry, who had bought them from Nye. "It took me years to get all those pictures," Charlie will tell me later. Eddy's Club was well-loved by its clientele, a legendary bar of its time. And Charlie's lives on in its wake. A poem hanging on the wall at the end of the bar by Missoula poet and longtime regular Dave Thomas pays homage to the old Eddy's Club, ending with a mention of writer Jim Crumley having an office here. Actually it was the office of one of Crumley's fictional detectives (and alter egos).

Charlie's was also the font from which Crumley, who liked to be around real people with tough lives, drew some of his characters. In the French film featuring Crumley (*The Way of the Road*), the writer describes coming here: "It's as if you'd given a party and everyone you liked showed up in a good mood."

Later I'll come in at eight-thirty in the morning to talk with Charlie. I had come in the day before hoping to catch him for an interview, and one of the many young, attractive, tough women who bartend for Charlie told me my best bet was to come in between eight and nine a.m. So I show up at eight-thirty and Charlie's got receipts and bookwork spread out on the bar in front of him, his glasses balancing halfway down his nose. He's not particularly interested in talking with me, but reluctantly agrees. Several regulars pour themselves a cup of coffee on their way in, and Charlie deals with a few suppliers while I talk with him.

He tells me he's been behind the plank for forty years, having started as a bartender for his father-in-law at Connie's when it was where the Rhino now sits. He said he worked seven days a week for ten years with one three-day vacation. He still works every day at this bar, but not nearly the hours he did before. I ask him if he always had female bartenders. He replies that he's had female bartenders his entire career. "I just get along with them better," he grumbles. "It just clicks."

Charlie's, like many bars, has a daytime and nighttime personality. One afternoon Dianne and I sat and chatted for a couple of hours. It was after the lunchtime run on the Dinosaur Cafe in the back and all that was left were the afternoon regulars, Dianne, and me. We were the only women in the bar, and Charlie, who dropped in briefly, immediately bought us a drink, having the bartender place the customary empty shot glasses in front of us to indicate we had one coming. Several regulars tried to engage us in conversation over the course of a couple of hours, most of them treating us special, something like women might have been treated in the Old West. It was endearing.

A second plank in the back is flanked with bar stools and behind that, the small sign of the Dinosaur Cafe, another Missoula landmark, serving tasty down-home Cajun-style cooking to the masses. Charlie's is the kind of place that anyone can come to for lunch and feel comfortable, alone or with friends, topping off the spicy food with a tap beer or a glass of water. I probably come here more often than any other Missoula bar, and the Dinosaur is likely the reason.

At night, the bar turns over. It has an atmosphere at once friendly, rambunctious, and dangerous. Like Eddy's Club, there's a feeling that about anything could happen. There's the old regulars, college students, river guides, professionals, pretty girls and gnarled veterans, skiing hotdogs and nerdy computer hacks, out-of-towners and inveterate locals. It's a place where people will still bet on six-man football teams—from tiny towns around Fort Benton—Geraldine and Highwood. Yet there's an edge to Charlie's that's hard to describe.

The general darkness of the place at night conjures up memories, for me, of Eddy's bartender Doug grabbing misbehaving men by the neck and throwing them out the back door. The pool table has seen its share of scuffles over the years and walking past it to the Dinosaur or the bathroom on a busy night still makes me a little nervous. Graffiti has always been a big thing in the restrooms, the women's at least. When I return from a restroom trip, Dianne asks me if I wrote on the chalkboard on the inside door of the women's stall. I said I had. She asked what I wrote. I admitted I wrote my meditation mantra. I couldn't think of anything else.

You know you're old when that happens.

The Rhinoceros
158 Ryman Street, Missoula
We push on to the Rhino, a bar loved by many and recommended to me by a few people along the way. It's been featured in at least one novel and it's a happy place

tonight. Known for its huge array of tap beers, the Rhino also has bartenders who are great mixologists, Dianne tells me, talking about a martini she recently enjoyed here.

Dave comes back to our table with shots of the bar's holiday nog, which warms Kelly up enough to tell the Maxville story. Kelly first courted me in the VFW bar in Maxville. This story is about how sixty-something George, a VFW regular, dealt with some young punks who kept trying to drag him into a fight. George was legendary strong, even in his sixth decade. In his youth he was a bar fighter, so he was not the person these two young men should have tried to lure into a fight. Of course, they didn't know that. They just saw this rather old man drinking a hole into the afternoon. I've heard the story a couple of times but Kelly's delivery tonight is better than usual. When he comes to the point in the story where George finally stands up, picks up one of the youngsters, and throws him at the woodstove in the corner of the bar, he's got us all in the palm of his hand. He ends with something I didn't know: "And that's when they went to gas heat at the bar."

I look around and find everyone totally engaged in conversation—a very jovial crowd. Signs of Snowbowl, Missoula's ski area, are found throughout the place, and I know this bar is popular with river guides. A Rhino head mount is bedecked with Christmas lights. Dave brings another round of Christmas nog, which soon prompts Kelly to buy a round of "real drinks"—shots of Crown

 The Rhino in Missoula is renowned for its expansive array of tap beers.

Royale. Ah well . . . it's on to the Top Hat, through the back door. We search for pavement amid the icy patches in a dimly lit alley. It all seems vaguely familiar.

The Top Hat
134 West Front Street, Missoula

Coming in the back door of this establishment is quite natural; I've probably entered this way as often as from the front. We amble in past the seating area, by the dance floor, to the front near the pool table. Lots of memories, including the wild night I had with my parents when I was still in college and they were probably younger than I am today. I somehow remember where we sat that night and how fun it was that Dad bought all the drinks.

I haven't been here in a few years and I've heard that there's no smoking at night now, but it takes a few minutes to realize how different the Top Hat is without smoke.

No band has been booked and it's a quiet night, so we find seats at the bar. Everything seems so different. First, the back bar. I never realized the Top Hat had such a classic back bar. Later someone will tell me it's because they always had so much stuff plastered on it. That's probably part of it, but I think it's also because there's no haze of smoke in the air. You can see everything—clearly. It's clean and almost airy tonight. I'm simply amazed. This bar, although staying pretty much the same, in some ways seems more different than any I've visited.

It's like it's the first time I've been here. Today's Top Hat suggests to me an old San Francisco saloon, with its large black-and-white photos filling the wall space, various seating nooks and levels, a large stage and dance floor, and towering ceilings.

Kelly and Dave immediately get into a pool game and one of them orders more shots. Just what they need. It's looking to be the beginning of the end of the night.

The Top Hat has been a Missoula landmark for years, well known for the great bands owner Steve Garr booked (sadly, the legendary Garr died suddenly in early 2009; his children took over the bar). It's always been popular with the college crowd, which suggests why it's slow tonight over winter break. Usually when I've been here over the years, the bar is three-deep with people. It's quite refreshing to just soak in the airy vibes with no one jostling you for position. But someone dumps the eight ball into a pocket and it's on to the Union Club.

Union Club

208 EAST MAIN, MISSOULA

The Union Club has music tonight and it's hopping, as it almost always is on a Friday night. Lack of college students only vaguely affects this bar, which is a magnet

 Patrons of the Top Hat are as likely to enter through the back door as through the front.

to music lovers and dancers on the weekends and a favorite haunt for a wide spectrum of locals of all ages. It's also a Democratic Party hangout and the place Democrats go to on any and all election nights.

Bartender Jeannie is in tonight, as she often is on busy nights, although she also works the bar weekdays. With her bouffant blonde hairdo and smiling face, she is the epitome of the classic barkeep—efficient, kind, firm when she needs to be, ready to listen—for a time—to any and all life problems. She tells me she's leaving in a few months, retiring from some thirty years behind the plank, moving to Boise to be near her son. The cavelike Union Club will lose its sun when she goes. The bar is deep with people and we don't need any drinks anyway, but she gives me a big smile as I wave hello.

Kelly and Dave are drawn to the pool table again. No surprise. They get into a doubles game with two men who seem to be dominating the table. Soon, a squabble ensues—something about bar rules and league rules. The guys insist on playing league rules. Dianne stands up to one guy, getting in his face, insisting that they should play bar rules. It seems she's a bit of a pool shark herself. The guy sticks to his guns, as does Dianne. I don't know what they're talking about, but I'm all for Dianne. But the guys seem to be in charge, as it's their table. And they're both apparently quite sober. Not much fun. Kelly, who can be a formidable pool player, misses one shot and his opponent runs the table.

Time for breakfast at the Ox. A few blocks in ten-degree weather is good for all of us. We move through the early morning north to the bright front lights of the Oxford, holding on to one another as if maneuvering on a ship deck.

The Oxford

337 North Higgins Avenue, Missoula

The bar is emptying into the cafe section as we arrive. After ordering, Dianne pulls me up to the plank to meet Beth, a woman with brown bangs, a ponytail, and a cheery demeanor that's hard to imagine at one in the morning in the Oxford. She's been tending bar at the Ox for twenty-one years. Beth tells me to come back later and she'll show me the book.

It's not like I really need a book to know about the Ox. Like all red-blooded western Montanans, it's been on my radar since I dropped into Missoula for college in the seventies. I've been coming here, off and on, since then.

When we moved back to Missoula in 1994, one of the first things I wanted to do was play poker in the Oxford. Kelly and I went one warm summer night and I lost eighty bucks before I could order my second drink. I often do well at poker with family and friends around a kitchen table, but I was clearly out of my league. Kelly took over with the money we had left, broke even, and we escaped that night intact.

I often came here in my twenties with Paul Smith, the boss of the Smith Gang, who always ordered brains and eggs for breakfast, what Shorty Hayden, legendary short-order cook coined as "He Needs 'Em." I'd usually get a "Stretch One and Pin a Rose on It" (a burger with a slice of onion). Boss and the gang were legendary barhoppers and I'm sorry he and his wife, Terry Minow, also known as Bullhead, weren't able to join me this time in my search. I'm thinking of them a few days after the Missoula pub crawl as I walk into the Ox at four in the afternoon.

The bar is busy, with all stools taken. I push through to talk with Beth and she hands over a book written by Steve Smith, *The Ox: Profile of a Legendary Montana Saloon*, published by Montana Pictorials in 1983.

I learn a bit I hadn't known about this bar, which has been featured in documentaries and national magazines. It's Missoula's oldest but there's debate over whether it was established in 1883 or 1888. It started on the northwest corner of Broadway and Higgins, but was moved in 1955, with patrons carrying the plank to this location, their drinks perched on the wood board, ready for wherever they landed. Since moving in 1955, it's never been closed. Open twenty-four hours. There are no locks for its doors.

I read about how Mike Mansfield would come here to chat with people—never drinking, but always ordering either the beef stew ("Under the Bridge") or the brains and eggs. The cooks would refrain from yelling "he needs 'em" when it was Mike ordering. There's a letter in the book to McFarland, the guy who owned the Ox from 1931 to 1955 from Congressman Mansfield, asking him what he thought of Mike's chances if he were to seek a seat in the U.S. Senate.

I look around and see, as with several Missoula bars, the place has been cleaned up, brightened. Large historical black-and-white photos line one wall—the U.S. Army's Black Bicycle Corps, who pedaled 2,000 miles from St. Louis, Missouri, to Montana in 1897 to test the practicality of military bicycling, Indian teepees spread below a towering mountain—now the University of Montana's Oval, loggers attaching huge stumps to a two-horse pull, cowboys wrangling a bronc. The cafe still has the impressive stainless-steel backdrop, the money cage. Poker machines line the hallway to the restrooms and the poker room. They have taken a toll on what used to be pretty much day and night poker games in the Ox. Now poker is more like a Monday through Saturday night thing.

Another member of the Smith Gang, Richard Smith, would often come to the Ox, long after he gave up drinking. Boss told a story at Richard's wake that says a bit about both the Ox and the man. Richard had a wonderfully wry sense of humor, was older than most of us, and would often sit away in a corner, smiling wistfully at our follies. His stories were always subtle, often ironic. A couple nights before he died, he had friends take him to the Ox for dinner. Richard told Boss how a young man approached their table, tattoos running up and around his arms, piercings all over the place, his hair spiked. He gave them menus and said, "Good evening. I'm Jim and I'll be your waiter tonight."

Missoula Club
139 WEST MAIN, MISSOULA

One day that snowy winter I lure my niece, Gena Ruth, out with promises of a burger for lunch. Destination? You guessed it.

The place is hopping as the clock nears one in the afternoon. All ages, all types, most of them here for the burgers. I pull up a stool and see bartender Shane looking quizzically at me as I try to get a focus, contemplating the line of drafts available. I finally opt for Moose Drool—it seems that kind of day—and catch up a little with one of my favorite bar men.

Shane is young but he's been at the Mo Club for eleven years. He's grown into his role here and is the guy I look for when I visit. Today he tells me that he's going to Barack Obama's inauguration. He knows Jim Messina, Obama's deputy chief of staff, who is also a major fan of the University of Montana Grizzlies. He saw Messina at a playoff game for the championship in Chattanooga, and Messina told Shane he'd get some tickets for him. Pretty cool, I say, and quietly add him to the list of people I know who are going, and who I vaguely resent.

I look around the old bar, trying to find anything different from thirty years ago. I've been here many times since then, of course, but haven't really made any comparisons. The Mo Club is a touchstone in the spinning orb of the world. It's not supposed to change.

The photos definitely haven't been changed or moved. We've still got Nasbey Rhinehart, an early Griz legend and trainer, smiling down on us. Connie Orr is

MISSOULA'S ORIGINAL BURGER JOINT

The Mo Club serves one of the best burgers you're likely to find. Fried right in front of your very eyes, spitting little wads of grease up toward the fan and creamy juice onto the grill. Your nose pulls in the thick, pungent aroma of frying meat. You long for that first warm, wet, absolutely satiating bite. The bartender flips the patty and then firmly presses it onto the grill. Minutes are hours. You're sure you haven't eaten in years. The bartender presses it one more time, then pulls it off the grill. He sets it on a golden toasted bun and then onto the plate. A little catsup, a touch of mustard, you cap it with the bun and close your eyes as you lift it to your lips. You bite through the just-crisp bun, into the slice of raw—so sharp, so ripe, so onion—and then to the Monterey jack cheese—deep and soothing—a pleasant forerunner to what comes next—the richly complex flavor of beef.

still stretching his right leg over the hurdle. Coach Jug Beck is there and Aldo Forte and Lou "Rock" Rockeleau. The Notre Dame logo in stark gold and black. The same black-and-white photos plastered over the archway wall, Griz memorabilia from almost before the start of time. The same small grill and overworked fan. The scarred and scuffed back bar—rode hard and put up wet. The same plea to save the plank: PLEASE DON'T CARVE ON OUR BAR. The pool table. One change is they've gotten rid of the tables and chairs in the side room, replacing them with stools and higher tables, which was a change my mother definitely didn't welcome and why she now is not as likely to go to the Mo Club for a burger. She truly hates those stools. The only other change I note today is the flavored Absolut vodkas that line a counter of the back bar.

I think of how packed this place gets before and after sporting events. How comfortable it is in the quiet times. How retired UM professors came here every week for years for burgers and pool. It remains the heart of Missoula's bar scene.

Ruthie joins me and she orders a Bloody Mary. We watch the grill for a few minutes. It's loaded with burgers and buns, so we know we might as well wait a little to order. People are recovering from Christmas, returning to the Mo Club as a way of reentering the world. There's a table of "Butte rats," as Butte-born Shane notes to another customer. I hadn't heard that term in a while and it's comforting somehow. Other people come in, a couple with a young son, another couple who look to be in their sixties, a college-age guy, more couples, more kids. Finally we order our burgers.

I ask Shane what happened to the Grizzlies at Chattanooga. A cloud runs over his face as he marches out a few reasons for the loss, most of them having to do with the game plan. It's clear it still stings. But he's going to Washington for the inaugural of the century. I guess he'll live. Ruthie and I tell him places to visit in D.C. A college student sitting nearby, clearly in need of some attention, hollers out, "And go to the Lincoln Memorial, sit in his lap, and tell him you want a pony."

The burgers arrive and we dig in. The horseradish-flavored cheese is a new option and I've come to enjoy that. A slice of raw. Nothing fancy. Everything good. Ahhhh . . . still one of the best burgers around.

Former President Bill Clinton dropped in for a burger earlier in the year after campaigning in the area for his wife, Hillary. Shane is wearing a T-shirt commemorating this stop that says "This One's on Bill." A *Missoulian* reporter had erroneously reported that Bill bought a shot for everyone in the bar that night. What really happened, Shane tells us, is that the bar bought the shots to celebrate Bill's being there. Shane said once the ex-president came in, he could see people all over the bar get their cell phones out and start calling friends. Within a matter of minutes, the place was crammed with a couple hundred people. Bill stayed for two and a half hours. He's always loved a crowd.

Last Run Inn
SNOWBOWL SKI AREA, MISSOULA

I look across the expanse of the Last Run Inn saloon at Missoula's Snowbowl ski area one late afternoon in early February and notice something. Everyone is happy. Very happy. In fact, most are in that advanced stage of euphoria that can only be produced by fresh powder, short lift lines, more snow on the horizon, friends in a similar state, and the comfort of a beverage of choice in a warm room.

It occurs to me that I've probably never been in an expanse literally *full* of happy people. If someone isn't happy, you certainly can't see it. I think the odds are that someone in this room has been diagnosed recently with cancer—or has a friend or relative who has been. That a few are ready to quit their jobs—or are facing the prospect that their bosses will do it for them. That some had a screaming argument with their children or spouses within the last twenty-four hours; that many are in physical pain and will be in more pain tomorrow.

And you know what? You wouldn't know it by them.

There's something about a ski hill bar that, at its best, is akin to a church. There's worship going on, alright, but it's an inward kind of celebration, with each person living out his or her hallelujah. You can't help but feel it at times like these: We are the chosen ones.

Or maybe it's just that we're all close to brain dead. Don't ask me my middle name after a good day of skiing. My mind is empty, swept clean, an icy breeze blowing the curtains on what used to be. What *is* may or may not be coming into focus. Even the frustrating wait at the bar is muted. Finally . . . "I'll have a Powder Hound Ale, please." Surprisingly, beer can be a sort of grounder on days like this.

There are many things I like about this bar that have nothing to do with skiing, like its Bloody Mary (picked best by the *Missoula Independent* every year for the past ten or eleven years), its wood-fired pizza, its celebration of gonzo skiing with the nude Gelande skier poster, and its general irreverence—the bumper sticker that says, REMOVE MISSOULA, RESTORE THE VALLEY. I also like the personal touches, like the photo of manager Garland's grandma riding a mechanized bull in some joint down south, or the sign put up when the bar is being cleaned—CLOSED FOR GROOMING.

The off-the-shoulder give-a-shit nature of skiers permeates the place. And I hope the feeling I had that afternoon while looking across the bar at all the happy faces is there when my life flashes in front of me.

I was nothing coming in but now I kiss my hand.

NOTES

1. Richard Erdoes, *Saloons of the Old West* (Avenel, New Jersey: Gramercy Books, 1997).
2. Kelly J. Dixon, *Boomtown Saloons: Archaeology and History in Virginia City* (Reno and Las Vegas: University of Nevada Press, 2005).
3. Montana News Association Inserts, Montana Historical Society (July 1918).
4. Elliot West, *The Saloon on the Rocky Mountain Mining Frontier* (Lincoln and London: University of Nebraska Press, 1979).
5. Robert L. Brown, "Saloons of the American West," *Denver Westerners' Roundup* 29 (March–April, 1973).
6. Ibid.
7. Samuel William Carvoso Whipps Diary, Montana Historical Society.
8. Erdoes, *Saloons of the Old West*.
9. Ibid.
10. Byron Cooney, "The Saloons of Yesteryear," *Montana American* (July 18, 1919).
11. Erdoes, *Saloons of the Old West*.
12. Ibid.
13. Ibid.
14. West, *The Saloon on the Rocky Mountain Mining Frontier*.
15. Ibid.
16. Erdoes, *Saloons of the Old West*.
17. Henry Bose Reminiscences, Montana Historical Society.
18. Dixon, *Boomtown Saloons*.
19. Erdoes, *Saloons of the Old West*.
20. Ibid.
21. *Helena Independent* (November 30, 1907).
22. Cooney, "The Saloons of Yesteryear."
23. Erdoes, *Saloons of the Old West*.
24. Larry Quinn, *Politicians in Business: A History of the Liquor Control System in Montana* (Missoula: University of Montana Press, 1970).

INDEX

ABOUT THE AUTHOR

Joan Melcher is a freelance writer and editor who lives in Missoula, Montana. She is a contributor to the *Miller-McCune* online and print magazines and her work has appeared in several other publications, including *Via, The Progressive, Environment, The Christian Science Monitor,* and *Montana Magazine.* When she can, she writes plays, many of which have received staged readings at the Missoula Colony. In 2003 her one-act play, *The Dog Confessor*, was produced at the Houseman Too Theatre in New York.

☞ The author with Sonny O'Day outside Sonny O'Day's Bar and Lounge, 1979.